ST CLAF

Christopher Stace read Classics at Cambridge, then taught at Christ's Hospital and Bradfield College. He has translated a variety of classical authors: Euripides for the BBC, Plautus for Cambridge University Press, and Sophocles for performances at the Royal Exchange Theatre, Manchester (*Philoctetes* in 1982; the two *Oedipus* plays in 1987). His publications include *Florence, City of the Lily* (Dent 1989), a celebration of his love of Italy, a translation of Jacobus de Voragine's *The Golden Legend* (Penguin 1998), and most recently a translation of Thomas of Celano's *First Life of Saint Francis of Assisi* (Triangle 1999).

St Clare of Assisi

HER LEGEND AND
SELECTED WRITINGS

CHRISTOPHER STACE

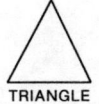

TRIANGLE

Published in Great Britain in 2001 by
Triangle
Society for Promoting Christian Knowledge
Holy Trinity Church
Marylebone Road
London NW1 4DU

British Library Cataloguing-in-Publication Data

A catalogue record for this book is available from the
British Library

ISBN 0 281 05294 8

Typeset by Pioneer Associates, Perthshire
Printed in Great Britain by
Omnia Books, Glasgow

CONTENTS

LIST OF ILLUSTRATIONS

Reproduced by kind permission of the Museo Francescano, Rome

MAPS

GENERAL INTRODUCTION

Writers search endlessly for good beginnings, and the author of the *Legend of St Clare* found one that strikes an appropriately reverberant note: *Admirabilis femina, Clara vocabulo et virtute . . .* 'This admirable woman, "Clare" alike in name and deed' (or, reading *clara*, with a small initial letter, 'of shining name and shining virtue'). At the very outset he makes the point that the saint's name is significant: Clare (Latin *Clara*, Italian *Chiara*) means 'bright' or 'shining' or 'illustrious', and from the moment her mother had her baptized with this name, after receiving a prophecy that she would give birth to a child who would brighten the whole world, Clare radiated a light of such brilliance that it not only illuminated her contemporaries but has shone undimmed through the 750 years since her death.

Until some 50 years ago, Clare lived very much in the shadow of her friend and fellow citizen St Francis; but growing interest in her own life and mission has made accessible an increasing amount of the source material, and with each passing year we can assess Clare's importance with a more informed appreciation. And it is impossible not to see this extraordinary saint and mystic in terms of light. Readers will quickly see how the motif of radiance permeates the writings not only of Clare's contemporaries (the bull proclaiming her sanctity begins with the ringing words *Clara claris praeclara*) but also of those who have been drawn to write about her since.

Clare was born in Assisi, Umbria, around the year 1194, and died on 11 August 1253. She entered religion aged about 18 and spent more than 40 years enclosed in her convent, and some 28 of those 40 years she was struggling with ill-health. Her name is of course linked inextricably with that of St Francis, whose ideal of gospel poverty she embraced and heroically put into practice. Yet she lived 27 years, the greater part of her adult life, after his death. Who was she?

What we know of Clare comes from the sworn evidence of those who knew her, from her own writings, and from other contemporary accounts. Of all the documents that bear on the life of Clare the two most important are the *Process of Canonization*, a document compiled at the instigation of Pope Innocent IV, and subsequently lost to us until as recently as 1920, and the *Legend* (an official biography, or Life to be read aloud: Latin *legenda*) composed soon after her death.

The *Legend of St Clare* translated in this volume was composed in prose. A *Verse Legend* exists, also of unknown authorship. It is an elegant and erudite composition in Latin hexameters, full of digressions and literary flourishes. It seems to be the work of some classically educated official of the Roman Curia, and it is dedicated to Alexander IV, who succeeded Innocent IV as pope in 1254. Interestingly, its author may be John the Englishman, papal legate in England, Scotland and Wales during the time that Innocent IV was pope. Though the *Verse Legend* was formerly thought to have been of later date than the *Prose Legend*, scholarly opinion now inclines to the view that it predates it. Because no reference is made to the canonization of Clare (which is the climax of the *Prose Legend*) it is reasonably assumed that the poem was composed at some point after Clare's death in 1253 and before her canonization in 1255. However, nothing startling is added by the poem to what we learn from the prose version; or perhaps (if we have the relative dates correct) we should say rather that the *Prose Legend* follows the *Verse Legend* closely, with a handful of small discrepancies of detail.

The *Process of Canonization* is a transcript of the evidence given to Bartholomew, Bishop of Spoleto, and the team of commissioners he appointed, at the behest of Innocent IV, to investigate the life and acts of Clare with a view to ascertaining her holiness.

The Process apparently lasted from 24 to 29 November 1253, and the bulk of the evidence was given by the community of St Clare's convent of St Damian's (San Damiano). Fifteen sisters gave their sworn testimony, and the abbess herself spoke on behalf of the whole community. Depositions were also made by three knights of the city of Assisi, by one lifelong friend of Clare's, and by one family servant of Clare's household. The evidence was given in Italian, and recorded by a notary in Latin. The text rediscovered and published in 1920 is not the original Latin one, nor even a copy of it, but a late fifteenth-century Italian version.

The primacy of this document must at once be clear: here we have the sworn testimony of those who knew Clare. These are the voices of her fellow sisters, the thoughts and feelings of her friends. The Church used an experienced prelate to conduct the interrogation, and the answers recorded, which clearly indicate his method of enquiry, prove that he was at pains to arrive at the truth. (Of course, this is the evidence of those who wished Clare proclaimed as a saint, but even so, the information it provides is unique and first-hand.) The author of the *Legend* certainly had this evidence at his disposal, though in order to be more sure of his facts he conducted his own interviews with those of Francis' companions still living, and with the Poor Ladies (as the sisters were called) at St Damian's. Some evidence he accepted, some he rejected: the result is the *Legend of St Clare, Virgin*.

Clare's own writings are also a valuable source of information. Clare was the first woman in the history of the Church to write a Rule for the religious life of other women, and this precious text (see pp. 79–104) when compared with the Rules imposed upon her by Cardinal Hugolino (1219) and Innocent IV (1247), in its adaptations and omissions and additions reveals to us in some detail the sort of life she was determined to lead, the life of absolute poverty preached by Francis which she lived until the day she died.

The *Rule* shows Clare's mind: to read it is to encounter a woman of great sanctity who was also a woman of large sympathy (there is nothing narrow about Clare's confinement). Clare was possessed of great common sense and practicality. All her life she fought for the Privilege of Poverty, and finally she emerged victorious – one saintly innovator, a single woman, against the reactionary prejudice of the whole Roman Church. Her *Rule* must be seen against the existing Rules of her times. In an attempt to regularize the life of the many new communities of religious women that were springing up in Italy and elsewhere (in the Lowlands, for example), the Fourth Lateran Council of 1215 had solemnly forbidden any religious life which did not follow one of the traditional Rules. Women religious had in practice to observe either the Benedictine Rule (which meant monasticism) or the Augustinian (which meant the canonical life). But these were men's Orders run by men, and in fact the monks were often extremely reluctant to undertake the responsibility for the spiritual care of women. Clare's *Rule* was the result of her search for an alternative.

We also gain a deep insight into Clare's mind and spirituality from the four letters that survive from her correspondence with Agnes of Prague. Agnes was a princess, the daughter of the King of Bohemia. She rejected offers of marriage (one, apparently, from no less a personage than the Emperor Frederick II) and, inspired by the preaching of the friars who arrived in Prague in 1225, she decided to leave the world. She established a convent of Poor Ladies on the lines of those at St Damian's (to which Clare sent five of her nuns from Trento) where she lived for 46 years until she died. She was later canonized.

Clare's *Testament*, her valedictory message to all her sisters, has traditionally been regarded as spurious, but French scholars have recently presented solid evidence supporting its authenticity. The matter is still far from certain. It is a work which recapitulates much that she had written elsewhere, and is intended as a statement of her wishes for all Poor Ladies after her death.

The *Legend* (chapter 45) states that on her deathbed Clare blessed her sisters, both present and future. Three very similar blessings, which survive in a variety of European languages, have been attributed to her.

It is only recently, since the middle of the twentieth century, and especially during the eighth centenary of her birth in 1993–4 that Clare's real importance, her own contribution to the ideals of Francis, has begun to be understood. There has been a steady growth of interest in Clare, and this growing interest has made available, in some cases for the first time, vital documents from which we are able to form a much clearer picture of Clare and her achievement in its historical context. She emerges as a torch-bearer, a prototype, a figure of real historical importance. Clare was living proof that the gospel life was not, after all, the prerogative of male spirituality. The times in which she lived witnessed many towering female figures: Clare's unique gifts and charism put her among the foremost of them.

The commissioners who conducted the first stage of the canonization process – the interrogation of witnesses – directed their investigation into four different stages of Clare's life: her *vita* (her secular life with her family at home); her *conversio* (her turning from the world and entering religion); her *conversatio* (her conduct during her 42 years at St Damian's); and her *miracula* (the signs which provided evidence of her sanctity). Leaving the miracles aside, this seems a sound enough framework for a brief survey of what we know.

Clare (Chiara) was born in Assisi in either 1193 or 1194 of noble and well-off parents: her father was a knight named Favarone, of the Offreduccio family, and her mother, herself of noble stock, was named Ortolana. The family house was in the fashionable heart of the city, on the Piazza San Rufino close to the basilica of San Rufino (the patron saint of Assisi). Ortolana, a pious woman who had been on the traditional pilgrimages abroad, is an important figure in the life of Clare: it was she who instructed her daughter (a willing pupil if ever there was one) in the ways of holiness, and later, probably after she was widowed, she followed her daughter into her monastery at St Damian's.

From her birth, 'from her mother's womb', Clare seemed marked out for a life of holiness. Even as a child she occupied herself with works of charity and was notably generous to the poor. She mortified herself by depriving herself of food and distributing it to the needy. She dressed modestly. She was devoted to prayer.

In her childhood Clare lived through troubled times: her city was torn with civil strife, with the struggles of the people against the nobles which characterize the period. She knew war and exile. During the war between Assisi and Perugia the Offreduccio family had to take refuge in Perugia. But we know little of her earliest years. As an aristocrat she would have received a good education. She was beautiful, and brought up with a view to marriage with someone suitably rich and powerful.

While Clare was still young the fame of Francis was spreading. The story of St Francis of Assisi (1181–1226) is almost too well known to retell. Francesco (originally Giovanni di Pietro Bernardone) was born to comfortably off middle-class parents, and had, after a conventionally riotous youth, undergone a total conversion. One day, around the year 1208, hearing the Gospel passage in which Jesus tells his disciples to leave everything (Matthew 10.7–19), Francis at last understood his mission and devoted himself to a life of poverty and prayer. He did not want to become a priest or a monk: he wanted to preach and save souls. Very soon he gathered around him a group of like-minded followers.

His situation was not without precedent. In the twelfth century, a time of great social and spiritual restlessness, there had been no shortage of itinerant preachers, some of them in accord with the authority of the Church, others regarded as heretics. A general dissatisfaction with the temporal power of the papacy and the worldliness of clerics engendered many different religious movements, and this process continued and proliferated throughout the twelfth century. When Innocent III became pope in 1198 he was understandably suspicious of these splinter-groups, and anxious to bring as many as possible under the wing of the Church. One such fraternity was the Humiliati of Lombardy, an order of penitents, both lay and clerical, who were devoted to works of charity and largely engaged in the wool trade. Innocent decided to organize them: he gave them a rule of life, and in 1201 formally granted them his permission to preach, a privilege he extended in 1207 also to the Catholic Poor Men. This was permission to preach moral sermons only (e.g. exhortations to a life of virtue), it should be noted, not doctrinal or scriptural sermons (which were the preserve of educated clerics).

Now Francis had no wish to challenge the ecclesiastical hierarchy: he needed the Church's recognition, and he wanted to distance himself and his followers from other superficially similar groups (like the Waldensians) who for one reason or another were regarded with suspicion by the authorities. He composed a simple rule of life, went to Rome and succeeded in gaining Innocent III's official approval. (For the story see Thomas of Celano's *First Life* chapter 33. This was oral approbation only, provisional and qualified, but with a promise of better things to come, if the friars' preaching bore fruit.) There he received permission 'to preach repentance to all men'.

When he returned to Assisi he and his friars began their preaching. He was a sensation. (His father had disowned him. Before the Bishop of Assisi Francis had dramatically stripped himself naked in a gesture of renunciation. All Assisi knew of the family scandal.) His inspired call to repentance and a return to gospel values struck a chord in the hearts of all who heard him. Noble and poor, clerks and laymen, men and women, everyone wanted to leave their homes and follow him.

Francis had already preached in St George's. In the spring of 1212 he gave a series of sermons in the cathedral. Clare heard him and was at once inspired by his new ideals. If she had been a man she must surely have joined him at the Portiuncula, a little church in the woods a couple of miles south-west of the city where Francis and his brothers lived. But she was a noblewoman; and though there were many penitential women's movements in evidence in the Italian peninsula and elsewhere in Europe, the itinerant and mendicant life was barred to her. Over a period of time Clare and Francis met. 'He visited her, and she more frequently visited him' says the *Legend* (chapter 5). Francis preached to her (one of his friars, Brother Philip, was also sometimes present) and in due course Clare decided to embrace a life of radical poverty. In the *Testament* Clare refers to her own 'conversion' as 'a short while after his [Francis'] conversion', but in fact some five years must have passed. (When Clare refers to her 'conversion', she means her passage from life in the world to a life in religion: she had been a devout Christian, of course, from her earliest years.)

The vivid and moving account of Clare's flight is best read in the *Legend* (chapters 7–8). She sought Francis' advice, and he told her what she must do. Doubtless Guido, Bishop of Assisi, knew exactly what was afoot when the young Clare came to Mass on that momentous Palm Sunday (either on 28 March 1211 or 18 March 1212) and lingered shyly behind when the others went up to receive their palms. In a memorable gesture of profound symbolism, Guido took matters into his own hands: he stepped down from the sanctuary and gave Clare her palm (the palm she still often carries when depicted in art). That night Clare fled from her family home and made her way to the Portiuncula, where Francis and his friars received her, and gave her the habit of penance and the tonsure. The same night (perhaps to protect her from interference by her family, who were bound to be outraged by her departure) she was taken off to the great Benedictine monastery of San Paolo delle Abbadesse at Bastia, a mile or so north. From there she went to the community at Sant'Angelo di Panzo at the foot of Monte Subasio, south-east of Assisi. (This was possibly a community of Beguines, a sisterhood of women living a religious life without vows and devoted to works of charity.) There she was joined by her sister Caterina, and successfully resisted all the attempts of her family to remove them by force. They were deeply offended by her unheard-of behaviour: suitably married to someone worthy of her rank, Clare might have cemented a valuable relationship with some important and powerful noble house, and the *maiores*, the aristocrats, needed constantly to close ranks in these troubled times. As it was, she had brought shame on them, and the whole city would disapprove. After all, she was not any ordinary young girl running away from home to enter a monastery: she was a noble young lady from a house well known in the area, and her family had important plans for her. But Clare, we are told, had sold her inheritance and given it to the poor, and in doing so she was announcing her divorce from her family. It had been her dowry portion, and now she was unmarriageable.

Then, finally, Francis sent Clare and her sister off to the tiny church of St Damian's, about half a mile south of Assisi, where she lived a cloistered life until her death in 1253. A community of sisters formed around her and came to be known as the Poor Ladies of San Damiano. In 1215, at Francis' insistence, Clare had reluctantly to accept the title of abbess, though in her writings she never uses the word of herself. In her *Rule* (or *Form of Life*, as she calls it) Clare goes out of her way to stress the humility and fairness essential to the abbess-figure, whom she sees not as an eminence, but simply as one among the sisters, living the ordinary life with the others.

Clare's movement spread far and wide, and many communities like that of the Poor Ladies sprang up elsewhere. Many daughter houses were founded in Europe in the thirteenth century. Wherever the Franciscan missionaries went they spoke of Clare's ideals and her community at St Damian's. Clare's sister Caterina, who took the name Agnese, went in 1219 to Monticelli near Florence to found a monastery of Poor Ladies, and was to found houses also at Padua, Venice and Mantua. And Princess Agnes of Bohemia in 1234 established her own monastery of Poor Ladies in Prague.

There are few hard facts about the more than 40 years Clare spent at St Damian's. (Significantly, her Life is told in 62 chapters compared with the 151 chapters of Francis' *First Life* alone.) Twice, we are told in the *Legend* (chapters 21–3), she saved St Damian's and her sisters from the bloodthirsty Saracen mercenaries in the imperial army: she is often depicted holding aloft a splendid post-Tridentine monstrance (which should in fact be a ciborium: see *Legend*, chapter 21, note 5), and scattering the enemy hordes. On one occasion, by her prayers, she saved her community and Assisi from the troops of Vitalis d'Aversa, the commander of the imperial army.

For the most part Clare lived out of the public eye in prayer and contemplation. We do not know for certain if she ever left the enclosure, though one delightful story – probably apocryphal, but conceivably based on a germ of truth – tells of her enjoying a meal with Francis and his friars at the Portiuncula. But we can surely infer a good deal of what her life must have been like from the *Rule* she composed.

At St Damian's Clare received the blind Francis in the spring of 1255, and it was there that he wrote the extraordinary and beautiful *Canticle of Brother Sun*. She made him an alb; she made him bandages to soak up the blood of his stigmata; she made him a pair of soft sandals. As he lay dying, Francis addressed his last will to Clare and her sisters, and in a touching farewell, his funeral procession stopped at St Damian's on Sunday 4 October 1226 on its way to St George's in Assisi.

From its very beginnings the little community at St Damian's was close to that of the friars; indeed, the Poor Ladies were sometimes known as the 'Lesser Sisters'. Francis had promised them his own support and that of his friars and their successors in perpetuity (though this obligation was soon to be a bone of contention among his Order) and all her life Clare struggled to ensure that this assistance was in fact continued. She always regarded the sisters and the friars as partners, as one family. Unable themselves to beg or preach, the Ladies (at least some of whom in those early days were indeed of gentle birth) plainly needed support, both material and spiritual. The Church was deeply concerned about the feasibility of women living in absolute poverty (between 1212 and 1220 there were many years of famine) and made repeated attempts to ensure the stability of their life by providing them with revenues of one kind or another, and with property to be held in common. In 1218–19 Clare was forced to accept the Rule of Cardinal Hugolino, which, broadly based on that of Benedict, was an attempt to regularize and provide pastoral and administrative assistance for the many communities of religious women living in Tuscany and Lombardy. But this Rule was not for Clare, and she resisted. Then, in 1247, Innocent IV imposed his own Rule, which, while avoiding reference to the Rule of Benedict, added considerably to that of Hugolino. But this, too, proved unpopular, and three years later he was forced to rescind it. Gradually Clare composed her own Rule, which was an adaptation of the Later Rule (1223) of the Friars Minor. Two days before she died, on 9 August 1253, papal confirmation of her Rule was finally granted in the bull *Solet Annuere*. She actually received the document on 10 August, and died next day. She had fought for two things: for the material and spiritual assistance of the friars, and for the right for herself and her sisters to live in utter poverty, without private property or property in common – something hitherto unheard of and, to the Church's way of thinking, in the case of women surely not only undesirable but a physical impossibility. Yet though physically frail (she had been ill since 1224) Clare was endowed with an indomitable spirit: her writings alone give an unmistakable impression of a vigorous, original mind. She had enormous strength of character. The confirmation of her Rule was a great personal triumph, and she died, it is said, clutching the precious document in her hand. At least for the time being the friars would continue to minister to the Ladies' needs. Against the inclination of the Church, and in defiance of popes, Clare had remained faithful to the original message of Francis.

Two months after her death, on 18 October 1253, Innocent IV gave Bartholomew, Bishop of Spoleto, the task of promoting the cause of her canonization, and in 1255, on a day close to the second anniversary of her death, probably 15 August, his successor

Alexander IV, who had been Cardinal Protector of the Poor Ladies, canonized Clare in the cathedral of Anagni in Lazio. Clare was the first non-royal woman for centuries to be raised to the altars. Her feast day was appointed for 12 August (she had died on the feast day of San Rufino, the patron saint of Assisi) and the bull of canonization was promulgated somewhere between 26 September and 19 October. Around 1260 the Poor Ladies moved from St Damian's to a new monastery in Assisi on the site of the old St George's, and with them they took Clare's remains. Clare's tomb was discovered in 1850 and on 23 September of that year her body was exhumed. In 1872 her relics were placed in an urn in the crypt.

Francis and Clare, Clare and Francis. The two are inseparable: the one is unthinkable without the other. Clare has been called another Francis, a mirror of the Franciscan spirit, Francis' right and left hand. Francis was her hero, her inspiration and her beloved friend. In the end Clare blessed her sisters in her own name and that of Francis, as if their partnership was finally complete, as if in the end they had become one person. And indeed Clare and Francis cannot be fully understood apart from each other. To inspire Clare God sent Francis. In return Clare sustained Francis and offered her life for the realization of his ideals. He inspired her, but then she was Francis' inspiration, because she was the feminine embodiment of his principles. But she was not only the most faithful interpreter of his ideals, she was an independent witness to their truth.

It has been suggested that without Francis Clare might not have had sufficient courage to break with her family and live a life of poverty. But she was always strong. When her family were attempting to take her back forcibly after her flight from home, we read of no intervention on the part either of Francis himself or of Guido the Bishop (whose word might have carried some weight). She was in fact on her own. Francis' attitude to women is often described as frankly misogynistic; certainly he was always suspicious of the temptations of the flesh and well aware of the dangers to which the brothers who visited women might be exposed. Clare states in the *Testament* that Francis encouraged the sisters to 'the love and observance of holy poverty' with 'many words', but apart from the story of his silent sermon to the Poor Ladies contained in Celano's *Second Life* (chapter 207) we know little of his personal associations with the Poor Ladies at St Damian's. Clare's life there was long and arduous, and the greater part of it was spent without Francis. Francis alone is simply not enough to explain her tenacity and her triumph.

Much has been written about Clare's relationship with Francis, and her dependence on him. Francis' influence on Clare's spiritual development is undeniable: she was his cherished disciple, his special 'little plant'. Clare's *Rule* and *Testament* eloquently acknowledge the fact. And clearly there was a loving friendship between the two, never expressly stated, perhaps, but obvious nonetheless. In the *Testament* Clare bases her defence of their joint ideal on 'our blessed father St Francis, our founder, planter and helper in the service of Christ'. She needed Francis' name and authority for diplomatic reasons, of course, and she would use it regularly for the support of her cause when the church authorities showed such a strong disinclination to allow her to pursue her radical new form of life.

Yet the fact that she lived most of her monastic life without him (in her letters to Agnes, for example, Francis hardly makes an appearance, except when referred to as a legislator) surely suggests that she deserves to be assessed independently. Clare developed in her own distinctive way, and though comparisons are difficult (because, for example, Francis and Clare tended not to be concerned with the same issues in their writings) certain clear differences between them do emerge. (For these insights I am indebted to Thaddée Matura's contribution to the introduction of *Ecrits*. See *Select Bibliography*.) For one thing, Francis concentrated on the God of the Trinity, whereas for Clare the deepest Christian experience was nuptial union with Christ (see the first and fourth letters to Agnes). Francis' spirituality tends towards its biblical and liturgical roots: Clare is more modern, more in touch with the new spiritual movements current in her time. Francis was the tragic, wounded, suffering saint: Clare seems more vigorous, more tenacious; she shows a more radiant optimism. She was a mystic with a profound prayer life, but always more down-to-earth, always more practical than Francis. What Francis saw as his ideal, Clare lived. Her writings reveal her as utterly feminine (her favourite imagery is of rich clothing, jewels, etc.), and she was not above using feminine wiles when diplomacy required it: yet she displayed a forceful, manly side to her nature that Francis lacked. He was not a gifted administrator: Clare proved that she was. He was the impractical visionary: Clare lived out his vision and showed how it could be achieved in practice.

Traditionally linked inextricably with Francis, Clare now emerges as a woman in her own right. She has her own unique place in the history of the Church. She has been called a link between the apostolic and the contemplative lives. In its uncompromising austerity her Rule went far further than any other that women had lived under before, and she and her sisters proved triumphantly that the path of 'highest poverty' was not closed to the female sex. She was an original, a revolutionary, and in many ways she seems a modern figure, a female ikon, a woman for our time.

The strict poverty of the Poor Ladies, the 'Second Order' of St Francis, became somewhat relaxed after the death of its leader and guiding light (as indeed had that of the Order of Friars Minor, after Francis died), and in the fifteenth century the Order was reformed by St Colette. Today the Poor Clares have a reputation as the most austere women's Order of the Roman Church. Most Poor Clare convents practise strict enclosure, and Clares, like their founding mother, are devoted to contemplation, to prayer and penance and manual work. What Clare began in that tiny community at St Damian's 800 years ago has survived and flourished. The Order can claim numerous saints (Clare and Agnes of Assisi, Colette, Catherine of Bologna, and Veronica Giuliani are just five of them) and many who have attained beatification. There have been Poor Clares who were martyred – in thirteenth-century Poland and Syria, during the French Revolution, and in sixteenth-century Menorca. In Clare's time houses opened outside Italy in Rheims and Béziers, in Acre in the Holy Land, in Tripoli and in Cyprus. In Spain alone 47 houses were established in the thirteenth century, the earliest of them in Pamplona. Convents sprang up in Bruges, in Moravia and Poland and Hungary and Croatia. By 1252 the Poor Clares were in England, too, first in Northampton, and then by the end of the century in London and Waterbeach. At the beginning of the twentieth century there was a total of 518 monasteries of Poor Clares throughout the world, with some 10,000 nuns. Today in round figures there are 950 monasteries with about 15,000 nuns.

In her uncompromising pursuit of perfection Clare drew women after her, and in the beautiful words of the Office of St Clare said by the Capuchins, she can rightly claim: '*Posuit me custodem in vineis: vineae florentes dederunt odorem.*' 'The Lord put me a keeper among the vines: the vines flourished, and gave forth their fragrance.'

SELECT BIBLIOGRAPHY

The Life of St Clare (including Rule), translated by Fr Paschal Robinson, OFM, Dolphin Press, Philadelphia, 1910.

Saint Clare of Assisi: Her Life and Legislation, by Ernest Gilliatt-Smith, Dent, London, 1914.

St Clare and her Order, A Story of Seven Centuries, edited by the author of 'The Enclosed Nun', London, 1918.

The Romanticism of St Francis, by Fr Cuthbert, OSFC, Longmans, London, 1924, pp. 79–124.

St Clare of Assisi, by Nesta de Robeck, Franciscan Herald Press, Bruce, Milwaukee, 1980 (reprint of 1951 edn).

St Francis of Assisi: OMNIBUS of Sources, ed. Marion A. Habig, Franciscan Herald Press, first published 1973; English edition SPCK, London, 1979.

Francis and Clare, The Complete Works, translated and with introduction by Regis Armstrong, OFMCap, and Ignatius Brady, OFM, Toronto, 1982.

In the Footsteps of St Clare, A Pilgrim's Guide Book, by Ramona Miller, OSF, St Bonaventure University, New York, 1993.

★*The First Franciscan Woman, Clare of Assisi and Her Form of Life*, by Margaret Carney, OSF, Franciscan Press, 1993. Includes a sensitive analysis and appreciation of the Rule.

★*Clare of Assisi*, by Marco Bartoli, Rome, 1989; translated into English by Sr Frances Teresa, OSC, Darton, Longman and Todd, London, 1993. The first thoroughgoing attempt at an objective biography of Clare by a professional historian.

★*Clare of Assisi, Early Documents*, revised and expanded edition (including the *Verse Legend* and *Rule*) by Regis J. Armstrong, OFMCap, St Bonaventure University, New York, 1993. All the relevant texts are translated with an introduction and notes.

La personalità di Chiara d'Assisi, by Roberto Zavalloni, Edizioni Porziuncola, 1993.

Clare of Assisi: A Biographical Study, by Ingrid J. Peterson, OSF, Franciscan Press, 1993. A vigorous attempt to rescue Clare from the shadow of Francis and establish her sainthood as valid in its own right.

Saint Clare of Assisi, by Sr Chiara Augusta Lainati, OSC, Edizioni Porziuncola, translated by Sr Jane Frances, PCC, 1994.

Santa Clara (1194–1994), Asociacion Hispanica de Estudios Franciscanos (AHEF), edicion di Agusti Boadas i Llavat, OFM, Barcelona, 1994.

★*Clare d'Assise, Ecrits*, Editions du Cerf, Paris, edn 2, 1997. Introduction, Latin text, translation, notes and index by Sr Marie-France Becker, OSC, Br Jean-François Godet, OFM, and Br Thaddée Matura, OFM.

★ Works of major importance

TRANSLATOR'S NOTE

Because the *Legend* of Clare is comparatively brief, it has been possible to include in this volume some of Clare's own writings.

For the *Legend* itself I have used the standard text of F. Pennacchi (1910); for the *Rule* and the *Letters* the text edited by Sr Marie-France Becker, OSC, Br Jean-François Godet, OFM, and Br Thaddée Matura, OFM, published under the title *Ecrits* by Les Editions du Cerf (corrected and enlarged edition 2, 1997).

My aim has been to produce a readable and accessible version; in the interest of intelligibility, therefore, I have occasionally taken some liberties with the Latin, but none that interferes with the sense of the text. (For the ease of the narrative, for example, I have not always translated every single word of an overfulsome honorific title.) On rare occasions, too, I have diverged from Pennacchi's text, but have listed these readings in the notes.

Where the psalms are referred to, the Hebrew numbering (followed by, for example, the Authorized Version) is given.

Various abbreviations have been adopted in the notes. The two Lives of St Francis of Assisi by Thomas of Celano are usually referred to as *First Life* and *Second Life*; *The Legend of St Clare* = *Legend*; the *Acts of the Process of Canonization* = *Process*; *St Francis of Assisi: Omnibus of Sources* = *Omnibus*; and *Clare of Assisi: Early Documents* = *Early Documents*. Marco Bartoli's biography *Clare of Assisi* is referred to simply by the author's name; and *Clare d'Assise: Ecrits*, by Becker, Godet and Matura (see *Select Bibliography*), is referred to as *Ecrits*.

ACKNOWLEDGEMENTS

Anyone wishing to read the primary sources relevant to Clare's life must consult *Clare of Assisi: Early Documents*, edited and translated by Regis Armstrong, OFMCap (see *Select Bibliography*). This indispensable compilation of sources has been constantly at my side and my debt to it is everywhere apparent, as it is also to *Ecrits*, the exemplary French edition of Clare's writings referred to above.

I must publicly extend my warm thanks to the staff of the library of the Franciscan International Study Centre at Canterbury, who have put their considerable resources at my disposal and made my work a real pleasure. I should also like to acknowledge my gratitude to Sr Frances Teresa, Vicaress of the Poor Clares at Crossbush, Arundel, who has somehow found the time and patience to answer my endless questions and to lend me relevant literature; and to Fr Gregory Shanahan, OFM, who, despite illness and the calls of business much more important, has once again responded warmly and wisely to my enquiries. I have had excellent advice: any errors that remain are therefore entirely mine. I must finally record my thanks to David Jones, who has tirelessly hunted books for me on the Internet; and to my old friend Freda Crockford, who has again read the text and made a number of helpful criticisms.

CHRONOLOGICAL TABLE OF EVENTS

—

1181/2	Birth of Francis (Giovanni di Pietro Bernardone).
1194(?)	Birth of Clare (Chiara di Favarone Offreduccio).
1200	Civil unrest in Assisi. Clare's family take refuge in Perugia.
1202–4	Francis a prisoner in Perugia. He becomes seriously ill.
1206	Francis renounces all his wordly possessions and begins to live at St Damian's.
1208	Francis hears the Gospel on St Matthias' Day and understands his mission.
1209	Francis goes to Rome and Innocent III gives him verbal approbation of his Rule.
1211	Failure of Francis' mission to Syria. Clare meets Francis.
1212(?)	On Palm Sunday Clare leaves the world and receives the habit from Francis at the Portiuncula. Clare stays at the monastery of San Paolo in Bastia then joins the women at Sant' Angelo in Panzo. April 3–4: Clare's sister Caterina joins her. Takes the name Agnes. April–May: Clare moves to St Damian's.
1212–15	Francis gives Clare a Form of Life.
1213	(Summer) Francis leaves for Spain, but gets no further than Provence.
1215	Clare accepts the title of Abbess of St Damian's. Innocent III agrees to grant St Damian's the Privilege of Poverty.
1218–19	Rule of Cardinal Hugolino.

The Cistercian Ambrose appointed as Visitor of the Poor Ladies.

1219   Francis leaves for the Holy Land (June) and preaches before the Sultan.
        Agnes, sister of Clare, appointed Abbess at Monticelli, Florence. Brother Philip becomes Visitor.

1220   Francis steps down as Minister General of the Order and appoints Peter of Catania. Ambrose reappointed Visitor.

1221   Elias becomes Minister General. Francis' First Rule.

1223   Second Rule of Francis.

1224   Francis receives stigmata at La Verna.
        Beginning of Clare's long illness.

1225   Francis stays at St Damian's and composes *Canticle of Brother Sun*.

1226   Clare's mother Ortolana enters St Damian's.
        Francis dies (3 October).

1227   Gregory IX entrusts care of Poor Ladies to Minister General of Friars.

1228   Francis canonized. Gregory IX renews the Privilege of Poverty (17 September) for the Poor Ladies of St Damian's.

1228–9 Philip the Long again Visitor of Poor Ladies.

1229   Clare's sister Beatrice enters St Damian's.

1230   Francis' body translated to new basilica built in his honour. Pope forbids friars to visit Poor Ladies without papal authority. Clare protests.

1232–9 Elias Minister General a second time.

*c.*1234 *First Letter to Agnes of Prague.*

1234–9 *Second Letter to Agnes of Prague.*

1238   *Third Letter to Agnes of Prague.*

1240   Invasion of Saracens.

1241   Vitalis d'Aversa attacks Assisi.

1247   Rule of Innocent IV for all Poor Ladies. Clare begins to compose her own Rule.

1250	Clare's illness worsens (November).
1252	Cardinal Raynaldus visits Clare, who asks him for approval of her Rule. He grants it (16 September).
1253	Agnes returns from Florence to be with Clare. *Fourth Letter to Agnes of Prague.* Two visits of Innocent IV to Clare (April and August). On her deathbed Clare receives confirmation of her Rule. Death of Clare (11 August). The Pope and his court attend her funeral. Her body removed to St George's. Pope initiates the investigation into the life and miracles of Clare. Process of Canonization takes place (24–9 November).
1255	15 August: canonization of Clare by Alexander IV at Anagni.
1260	Poor Ladies remove to Sa Chiara, Assisi. Translation of Clare's body there.
1850	Clare's body discovered. The sarcophagus opened.
1872	Her remains transferred to crypt of basilica.
1893	Discovery of Clare's *Rule*.
1920	Discovery and publication of the *Process of Canonization*.

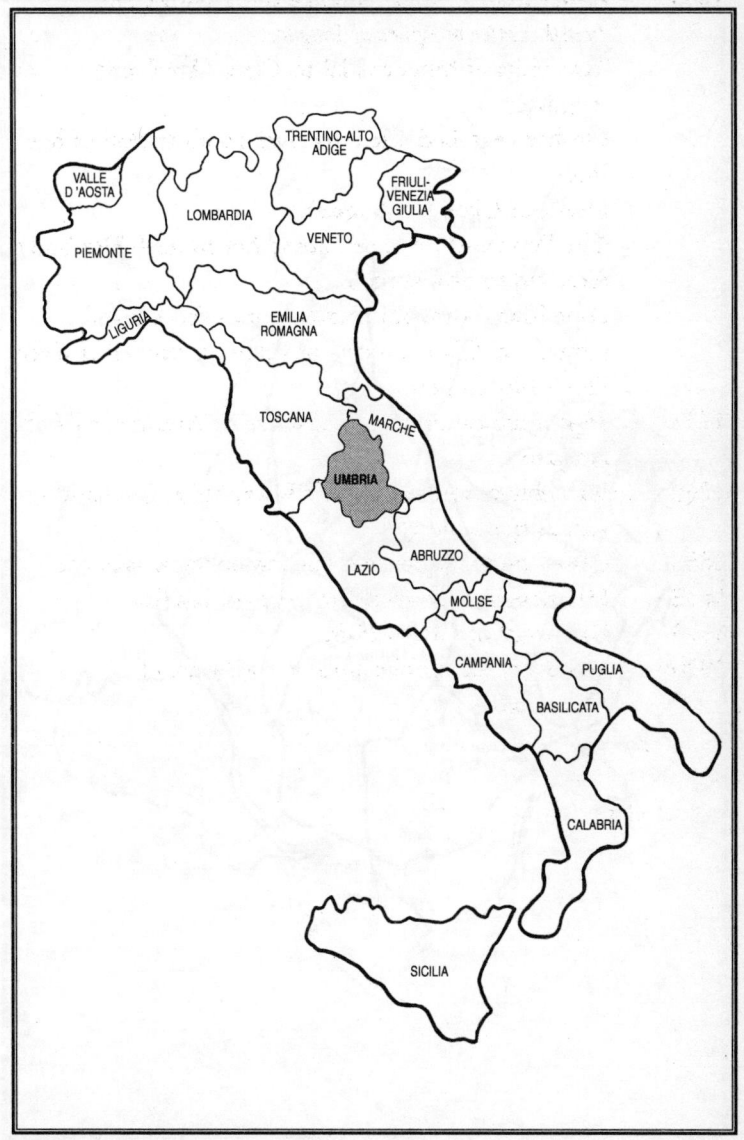

Map 1: UMBRIA *in relation to the other provinces of Italy*

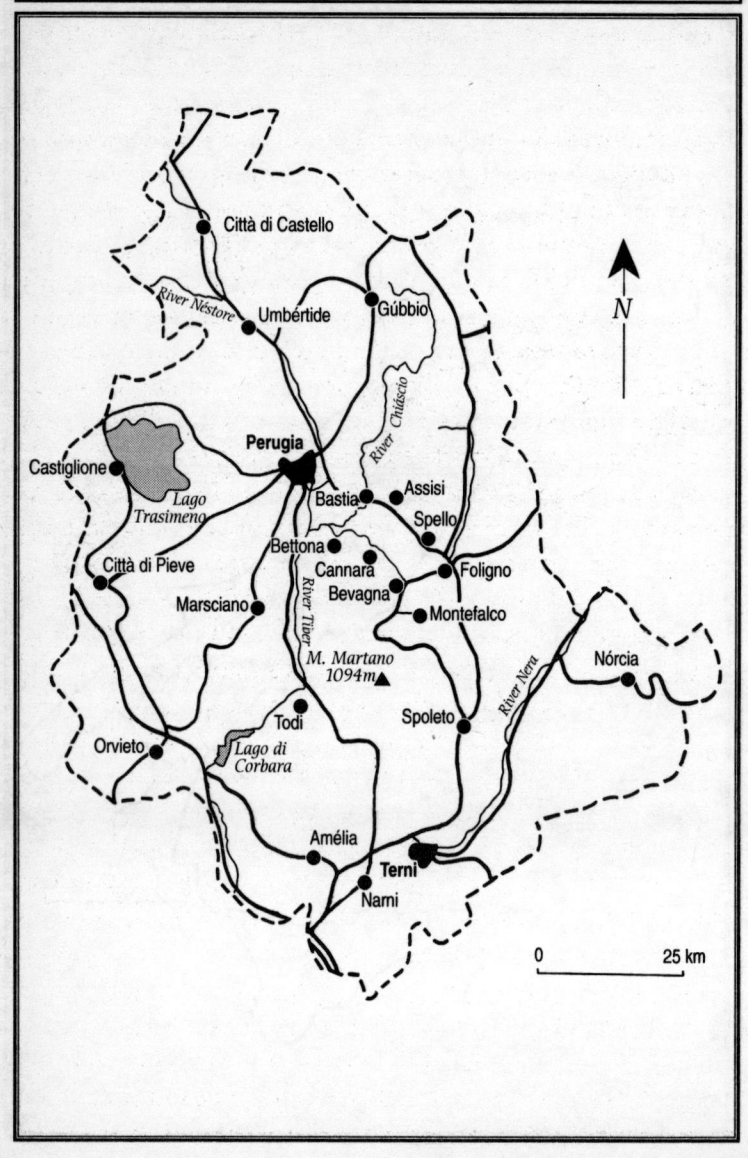

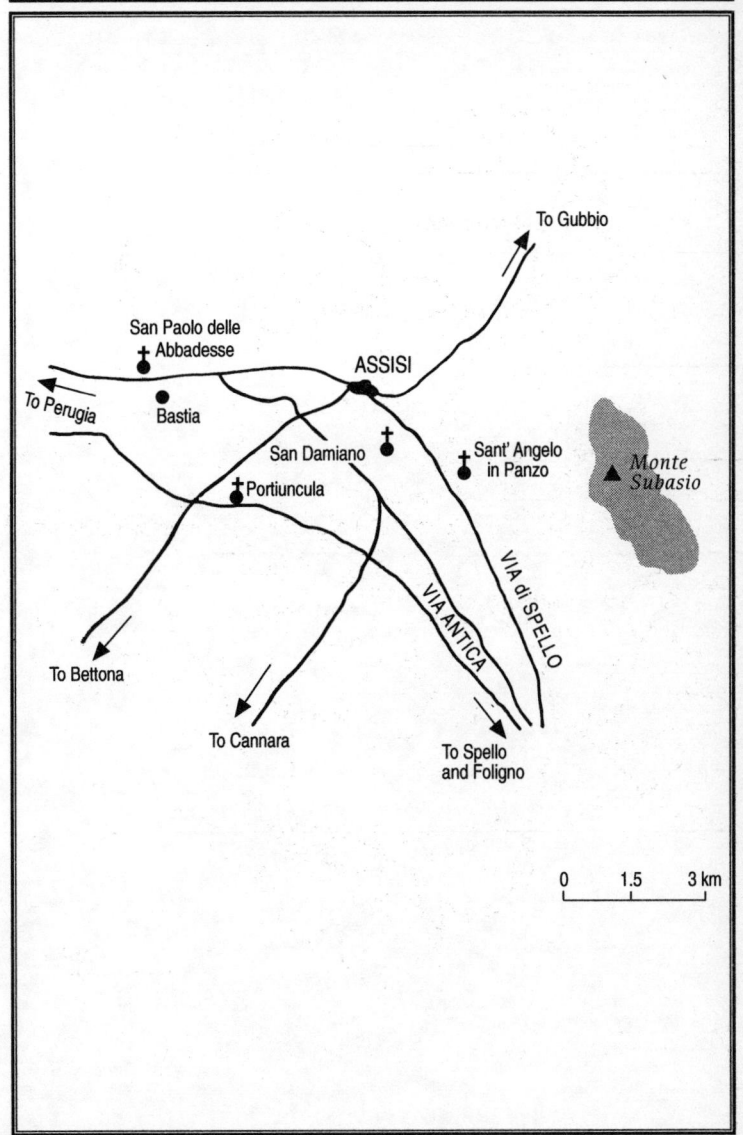

Map 3: ASSISI and environs

To Gubbio

San Paolo delle
✝ Abbadesse

ASSISI

● Bastia

To Perugia

San Damiano
✝

✝ Sant' Angelo
● in Panzo

Monte
▲ Subasio

✝
● Portiuncula

VIA di SPELLO

VIA ANTICA

To Bettona

To Cannara

To Spello
and Foligno

0   1.5   3 km

PART I

The Legend of St Clare

INTRODUCTION

The authorship of the *Legend* is unknown, but generally held to be Thomas of Celano, who had composed the *First Life* of St Francis at the command of Pope Gregory IX, then later a *Second Life*, adding material which for one reason or another had not been included in the earlier account. Various other candidates have been proposed, including St Bonaventure himself, Minister General of the Order of Friars Minor from 1257 to 1274, and author of the *Major Legend* of St Francis which was intended to replace Celano's earlier accounts and become the official Life. In the absence of firm evidence, and despite the determined resistance of at least one scholar at the forefront of Franciscan studies, Celano is still generally regarded as the most likely author.

In telling Clare's story, the author follows the traditional structure of the *First Life* of Francis. It is divided into two parts: the first covers the period just before Clare's birth up to her death; the second contains an edited list of the miracles worked through her intercession after her death, and ends with her canonization. The author clearly bases his information on the *Acts of the Process of Canonization*, though, as he is at pains to inform us in his prologue, he also conducted his own interviews with those followers of Francis still living and with the sisters at St Damian's, in order to make doubly sure of his facts, and to fill some of the gaps in the defective accounts already available to him. Even so, the facts are fragmentary, and the *Legend* as a result is slight: it is less than half as long as even the *First Life* of Francis. In itself this speaks volumes about the difference in the lives led by Francis and Clare.

But, like the *First Life* of St Francis, the *Prose Legend* of Clare (referred to in the notes simply as the *Legend*) is hardly biography in the modern sense: its author is concerned solely to establish

Clare's sanctity; he sets out her claims to sanctity, and his climax is the Church's recognition of her sanctity. The *Legend* was written to present Clare as a model of sanctity; its aim was the edification of Clare's spiritual daughters and of people generally. It describes her life as holy from its very beginnings, her death as holy, and her canonization as official acknowledgement of the fact. It is in fact hagiography rather than history: it does not as a rule follow the chronological order of events, and only one date, that of Clare's canonization, is given in the entire work. Time is handled in cavalier fashion, and events are grouped under various headings as the author deals with this or that aspect of the saint's life and character.

Some of the miracles recounted may strike modern readers as not only improbable, but even silly, yet no-one can doubt that the author has recorded them sincerely, and intends them to promote the fervour of the faithful. Our author is no purblind simpleton. He is an educated man, concerned to convey to the reader his theological insights. At the beginning of Part II, the section dealing with the miracles, he firmly declares his belief that the true proof of sanctity is not in wonder-working, but in holiness of life and in good works (see chapter 49). He is also capable of writing a Latin which can at times scale great heights of lyricism.

PROLOGUE

As if old age were oppressing a weary world, the eyes of its faith were growing dim: its moral direction was faltering, and its strength to perform manly deeds was fading; indeed, men's vices were as degenerate as the times in which they lived.[1] Then it was that God, the lover of mankind, from the hidden depths of his pity brought new forms of religious orders into being, and provided through them both a support for the faith and a standard for the reform of morals. I should without hesitation speak of these modern fathers and their true followers[2] as luminaries of the world, guiding lights, spiritual masters, men in whom the brightness of noontide has irradiated the earth at evening so that he who walked in darkness should see the light.[3] Nor was it fitting that help should be denied the weaker sex, which, once caught in the whirlpool of passion, was drawn to sin by a desire no less intense, and impelled towards it by its greater frailty.[4] For this reason the good Lord brought into the world the venerable virgin Clare, and in her kindled a brilliant light for all women, Clare whom you, most blessed Father,[5] have set upon a lamp-stand to give light to all in the house,[6] and moved by the greatness of her miracles have enrolled her in the number of the saints. We honour you as the Father of these Orders, we acknowledge you as their Patron, we embrace you as their Protector, we venerate you as their Lord: and though the supreme direction of the mightiest ship in creation rests upon your shoulders, it does not prevent you from showing a deep and anxious concern for smaller vessels too.[7]

It has pleased your Lordship to impose upon me, in my insignificance, the task of surveying the life[8] of St Clare and composing her Legend[9] – an undertaking which my want of literary skill would certainly cause me to shrink from,[10] had not the order been placed before me repeatedly and on papal authority. So, bracing myself to obey, but considering it inadvisable to rely on the defective accounts at my disposal, I approached the companions of blessed Francis and the community of the Virgins of Christ itself, reflecting often on the fact that no-one in olden times was permitted to write history except those who had witnessed the events themselves or had received their information from eyewitnesses.[11] When they, in the fear of the Lord and with due regard for truth, had given me a fuller account of the facts, I put down some of the material I had gathered, though rejecting a good deal more, and wrote this in a simple style so that, while the virgins will delight in reading of the great deeds of Clare, people of lesser intelligence may not find the meaning obscured through flowery language. So let men follow the new disciples of the Lord incarnate; let women imitate Clare, image of the Mother of God, the new leader of womankind.[12] But just as in you, most holy Father, rests full authority to correct, abridge or add to what I have written, so is my will subordinate, submissive and deferential to you in all things.

May the Lord Jesus Christ prosper you, now and for ever. Amen.

NOTES

1 The author begins in his elevated, poetic style. The *Legend* is throughout partly factual, partly authorial commentary. The factual evidence is firmly based on the Process of Canonization: the theological commentary seems to represent the author's own contribution.

2 St Francis and his disciples.

3 Isaiah 9.2.

4 The secular attitude to women in medieval times was one of suspicion, and this was to an extent reflected in the Church's thinking. Woman was the cause of original sin, and the supposed weakness of women meant that religious women had to be enclosed.

5 Pope Alexander IV, formerly Protector of the Order, who canonized St Clare.

6 Compare Matthew 5.15.

7 The mighty ship is the Church; the smaller vessel the community of St Clare.

8 Literally, her 'acts'.

9 A 'Legend' meant an official biography to be read aloud (Latin *legenda*).

10 A conventional disclaimer: the author is clearly an educated man and a skilled exponent of this genre.

11 The author based his *Legend* on the evidence produced by the official investigation into the life and miracles of Clare, but also went in person to question people who had known Clare personally. Several of Francis' companions were still living: Angelo and Leo, for example, who with Juniper were at Clare's side when she died (see chapter 45). The 'Virgins of Christ' were the Poor Ladies at the monastery of St Damian's.

12 All the sisters of St Damian's giving evidence at the Process of Canonization considered Clare to be the holiest of women, second only to the Virgin Mary. The word translated as 'image' means literally 'footprint'. The phrase 'footprint [= copy] of the Mother of God' occurs in a hymn to Clare composed by Alexander IV.

PART ONE

HERE BEGINS THE LIFE OF THE HOLY VIRGIN CLARE

⌐−⌐

First: Her Birth

⌐−⌐

1 Clare, this admirable woman, of shining name and shining virtue,[1] was born to an illustrious family of the city of Assisi. She was first a fellow citizen of blessed Francis on earth, and then she reigned with him in heaven. Her father was a knight,[2] and indeed all her relatives on both sides were of knightly descent. Her family was well-to-do and, as was customary in her native city,[3] owned extensive property. Her mother, Ortolana,[4] who was to bear such a fertile seedling in the garden of the Church, herself brought forth a rich harvest of her own good fruit. For though she wore the yoke of marriage and was tied to the household and its concerns, she gave all the time she could to divine worship and was tireless in her devotion to good works. Indeed, in her piety she crossed the sea on a pilgrimage, and visited the places which he who was God and man had hallowed with his sacred feet, and at length returned home full of joy. She also went to pray at the shrine of St Michael Archangel,[5] and with even greater devotion visited the churches of the Apostles.

2 What more need be said?[6] A tree is told by its fruit,[7] and the fruit owes its goodness to the tree. A richness of divine favour was in the root, so that an abundance of holiness might follow in

9

the little branch it put forth. When in due course Ortolana became pregnant and the time of her delivery was close, she was kneeling before the cross in a church and earnestly beseeching the Crucified that he might help her safely through the peril of childbirth, when she heard a voice saying: 'Do not be afraid, woman, for you will give birth in safety to a light which will outshine light itself.' In accordance with this prophecy, when her child was born, then born again in Holy Baptism, Ortolana had her named Clare,[8] hoping that the brightness of the light God had promised in some way be fulfilled according to the gracious purpose of his will.

NOTES

1 In the opening words the author trumpets the significance of Clare's name (Latin *clara*), which means 'bright', 'shining', 'glorious', 'illustrious'. This fact is alluded to constantly in the *Legend*.

2 Clare's family, which boasted seven knights, was not the greatest of Assisi, but was certainly aristocratic. (See *General Introduction*.)
The head of her family was her uncle Monaldo (see chapter 25).

3 The Latin could also be taken to mean: 'and had abundant means in relation to the general condition of the country'.

4 Her name is derived from the Latin word for garden (*hortus*), and *ortolana* in Italian means gardener. Clare is regularly referred to as the 'little plant' of St Francis.

5 The celebrated sanctuary of St Michael on Monte Gargano in Puglia.

6 This phrase (cf. the start of chapter 6) does not occur elsewhere in the writings of Thomas of Celano, a fact which has been made much of by those who contest his authorship.

7 Compare Matthew 12.33.

8 This was in 1193 or 1194, and Clare was baptized at the same font in the cathedral church of San Rufino as St Francis had been. Clare was an uncommon name then, as was Francesco: now, like Francesco, it is extremely popular.

Her Life in Her Father's House

3 No sooner had the little Clare seen the light of day[1] than, appropriately enough, she began to shine with a radiance of her own in the darkness of the world, and during her tender years she was conspicuous for her virtuous conduct. First she received with docile heart the rudiments of the faith from her mother's lips, and as the Spirit kindled her and shaped her inwardly, she became known as a most pure vessel, a vessel of graces. She freely stretched out her hand to the poor, and from the affluence of her home supplied the wants of many.[2] And so that her sacrifice might be the more pleasing to God, she deprived her own young body of choice foods, and sending them out secretly by means of intermediaries, she would satisfy the hunger of orphans. So from her infancy, as mercy grew with her,[3] Clare showed a compassionate nature, and felt pity for the plight of the poor.

4 She was deeply devoted to the practice of holy prayer and so often bathed in its goodly fragrance that little by little she came to embrace a life of religion. When she had no beads to turn and number her paternosters, she used a handful of pebbles to count her little prayers to the Lord.[4] When she began to feel the first pangs of divine love, she realized that the fleeting show of wordly beauty should be spurned, for she had been taught by the unction of the Spirit to set a low price on things of low value. Hidden beneath her costly and soft clothing she wore a hair-shirt,[5] to the outer world seeming like a flower in bloom, while inwardly putting on Christ.[6] At length, when her family wanted to marry her to a nobleman,[7] Clare would not hear of it, but pretending that she would marry someone at a later date, she entrusted her virginity to the Lord. Such were the tokens of her virtue in her father's house, such the first-fruits of her spirit, such the beginnings of her holiness. So Clare, bathed as she was in so great a fragrance[8] – just as a container of sweet spices, even though closed, betrays its contents – became known by the odour

of her sanctity. Unknown to her, she began to be praised by her neighbours, and when the truth of her secret life became known, her reputation for goodness spread widely among the people.

1 Literally she was 'brought into the light', another play on Clare's name and its associations.
2 Compare Proverbs 31.20; 2 Corinthians 8.14. According to one witness (*Process* XVII 7) Clare also sent out money for the bodily needs of the men working on St Mary of the Portiuncula. This may well have included Francis.
3 Compare Job 31.18.
4 Prayer beads had long been in use as a means of counting prayers. In medieval church Latin they were known as paternosters.
5 According to the old manservant of Clare's household (*Process* XX 4) this was a 'rough garment', which would merely be one of undyed wool. Here it becomes a prickly pigskin, emblem of heroic self-mortification (Bartoli 34).
6 Compare Romans 13.14; Galatians 3.27.
7 Two witnesses who knew Clare well stated under oath that because she was beautiful many of her relatives wanted to marry her.
8 The theme of Clare's sweet fragrance is recurrent. Saints have traditionally been associated with an 'odour of sanctity' after their death, and some have been known to exude a sweet scent during their lifetime. Compare chapter 10, and Song of Solomon 1.3. Throughout the Song of Solomon, perfume is symbolic of the charms that intoxicate the heart.

Her Acquaintance and Friendship with the Blessed Francis

5 Hearing of the then famous name[1] of Francis, who, like a new man[2] was renewing with new virtues the way of perfection forgotten in the world, Clare was moved by the Father of Spirits (to whose overtures both had responded, though in different ways) and at once longed to hear and see him. And Francis, impressed by the far-reaching fame of such a virtuous young lady,

was equally eager to see and speak with Clare. For he was ravenous for spoils, and having come to plunder the kingdom of this world, he hoped he might somehow snatch this noble prize from the wicked world[3] and claim her for his Lord. He visited her, but she more often visited him,[4] arranging the times of her visits so that their holy purpose should not be discovered by anyone nor become the subject of malicious gossip. The young Clare would leave her father's house with just one companion, a close friend, and meet the man of God in secret; and his words seemed to her to be on fire, his deeds more than human. Father Francis encouraged her to despise the world,[5] demonstrating in vivid words the barrenness of earthly hopes and the deceitfulness of its beauty. He inspired her with the joys of espousal to Christ, urging her to preserve the pearl of her virginal purity for the Blessed Spouse whom love made man.

6 What more need be said? The most holy father was so persuasive, and so skilful in his role as faithful bridesman,[6] that Clare did not delay long before giving her consent. And at once a vision of the eternal joys was revealed to her, such that at the sight of it the very world became worthless, and with desire for it she melted away, and for love of it she panted with desire for her heavenly marriage. Burning with celestial fire, Clare so utterly disdained the glory of earthly vanity that nothing of worldly acclaim any longer clung to her affections. Moreover, in terror of the temptations of the flesh she now determined to know nothing of the sin of the marriage bed; she desired to make of her body a temple for God alone, and strove by her virtue to prove worthy of marriage to the Great King. From that moment she entrusted herself totally to the counsel of Francis, and regarded him, after God, as the guiding light of her life. Thereafter her soul hung upon his holy admonitions, and she received with eager heart whatever he told her of the good Jesus. She was already wearied by the glitter of earthly adornment and counted as dung everything prized by the world: her only desire was to win Christ.[7]

13

1 At this time his Rule had been granted oral approbation (1209), and his followers were preaching everywhere. Francis himself preached first in St George's, then was invited to speak in the cathedral, where crowds massed to hear him.

2 Compare Ephesians 4.24. Francis was a reformer. In living the gospel life he was reminding the world of a long-lost holiness.

3 Compare Galatians 1.4, which has language somewhat similar.

4 Who took the initiative in these clandestine meetings, which went on for some years? Clare's sister Beatrice says (*Process* XII 2) it was Francis: Bona de Guelfuccio, the close friend who accompanied her on these visits (*Process* XVII 3) says Clare, and our author seems to imply the same. Clare always had a strong spirit of initiative.

5 Bartholomew of Pisa (*c.* 1260–1347) tells us that Francis, in order to test the sincerity of Clare's vocation, told her to go round the city in sackcloth begging alms. But Clare was a noblewoman, and this would have been asking for trouble from her family before it became absolutely unavoidable.

6 The 'bridesman' (Latin *paranymphus*, a Greek word) was the groom's go-between.

7 Compare Philippians 3.8, where Paul says: 'I count [all things] but dung, that I may win Christ.' See Letter III to Agnes of Prague, n. 11.

How She was Turned from the World by Blessed Francis and Entered the Religious Life

7 Lest the mirror of her unblemished soul might be further spotted by the world's dust or earthly contamination spoil her uncorrupted youth, the good father at once made haste to take Clare from the darkness of the world. The solemnity of Palm Sunday[1] was at hand when the young Clare went with fervent heart to Francis to ask him what she should do to accomplish her withdrawal from the world, and how it might best be done. Father Francis told her that on the feast day she should go to receive her palm dressed in her finery together with everyone else, and that

Palm Sunday 1212 (?). Bishop Guido hands Clare her palm

the following night she should decamp[2] and convert her worldly
joy into mourning for the Lord's Passion. So when Sunday came,
resplendent in her festive garments among a throng of ladies
young Clare entered the church with the others. Then something
happened that was portentous indeed: as the others eagerly went up
to receive their palms, Clare out of shyness remained motionless
in her place, and the bishop[3] came down the steps to where she

15

stood and placed a palm in her hands.[4] That night Clare made ready to carry out the saint's command, and, suitably accompanied,[5] she embarked upon the flight she had so longed for. And since she did not wish to leave by the usual door she broke open another, with miraculous strength, broke it open with her own hands, a door which was walled up with a mass of beams and stones.[6]

8 And so, leaving behind her home, her city and her family, she hurried away to St Mary of the Portiuncula,[7] where the friars, who were keeping a vigil at their little altar of God, received the virgin Clare with lighted torches. Once there she cast aside the dross of Babylon and formally divorced herself[8] from the world: there her hair was shorn by the friars[9] and she laid aside all her elegant finery. For it was not fitting that an Order of virginity springing up in these latter days[10] should flower in any other place than here, in the sanctuary of her, the first and most worthy of all, who alone was a Virgin and Mother. This is the place[11] in which a new army of the poor, under the leadership of Francis, had its happy beginnings, so that it might clearly be seen that it was the Mother of Mercies who was bringing to birth both Orders under her own shelter.[12] And as soon as the humble handmaid Clare had received the habit of holy penance before the altar of blessed Mary, and, as if before the throne of this Virgin, had been espoused to Christ, Francis at once took her off to the church of St Paul[13] to remain there until the Most High should provide some other place.

NOTES

1 A symbolic setting, carefully chosen. The palm is the emblem of victory, and Clare is often depicted holding a palm. The date is generally thought to have been 28 March 1211; but some put it one year later, when Palm Sunday fell on 18 March.
2 Compare Hebrews 13.13: 'Let us go forth therefore unto him without the camp, bearing his reproach.' Paul refers to the banishment of Jesus beyond the city walls.
3 Guido II, Bishop of Assisi 1204–28.
4 The gesture has been variously interpreted, but Guido was surely aware of what was planned.

5 The Latin *cum honesta societate* ('in virtuous company') could imply one or more companions. Traditionally Pacifica was held to be Clare's sole companion in her flight, but she does not mention the fact in her evidence at the *Process*. Quite possibly a few of Francis' brothers served as escort. Interestingly, the *Verse Legend* says that Clare went alone.

6 The doorway through which Clare is thought to have escaped can still be seen. It may have been a 'porta di mortuccio', walled up because a corpse had recently been carried through it. If so, Clare's act acquires a deeper symbolism.

7 St Mary's, a humble little chapel on a plain below Assisi, had been given to Francis by the Benedictines of Monte Subasio. It became the site of the first convent, and the cradle of his Order.

8 Literally 'issued a bill of divorce', a rather daring metaphor, as divorce was the man's prerogative. This nuptial terminology is a recurrent motif of the *Legend*.

9 Five different witnesses in the *Process* state that Francis himself carried out the tonsure, but our author makes it a communal act (perhaps because he was uncomfortably aware of just how extraordinary such an act was: after all, Francis was not a bishop, nor a priest, perhaps not even at this time a deacon). The tonsure marks the beginning of a religious, penitential life, and expresses separation from the world.

10 Literally 'awakened towards evening'. There was a pervasive feeling among the devout that mankind was living in the twilight of the world.

11 'Place' (Latin *locus*) is regularly used to denote one of the early Franciscan convents.

12 Literally 'in her own inn'. Just as Mary gave birth to Jesus at an inn (Luke 2.7), so, appropriately, the Portiuncula gave birth to the First and Second Orders of St Francis.

13 San Paolo delle Abbadesse, a rich and important Benedictine monastery at Bastia, two miles west of Assisi. San Paolo had been granted rights of asylum by Innocent III in 1201.

———

How She was Persecuted by Her Kinsfolk, but Persevered and Stood Firm

———

9 When the news reached her relatives they were heartbroken; they condemned both what she had done and was proposing to do, and banding together as one they ran to the convent in a

forlorn attempt to get her back. They resorted to violence, used wicked arguments to poison her mind, and made her fulsome promises to persuade her to give up this shameful behaviour,[1] which was unworthy of one of her upbringing and without precedent in the area. But Clare took hold of the altar cloths and bared her shaven head, declaring that nothing would ever separate her from the service of Christ. And the more her family warred against her, the more her courage grew, and her love, tried as it was by the insults she suffered, lent her strength. So, although for many days she had to endure these attempts to come between her and Christ, and her relatives tried to obstruct her decision to lead a life of holiness, her spirit never gave way, her fervour never diminished.[2] But, amidst this storm of abuse and hatred, she schooled her heart to hopefulness until finally her relatives gave up the struggle and held their peace.

10 After a few days, Clare went to the church of St Angelo in Panzo,[3] but since her mind was not completely at rest there, finally, on the advice of blessed Francis, she moved to the church of St Damian.[4] There, it was as if she had at last found a secure anchorage for her soul. She no longer wavered or thought of moving elsewhere; she did not hesitate because of the cramped conditions, she had no fears for its loneliness. This is the church Francis worked so feverishly to repair, and to whose priest he had offered the money for its restoration.[5] It was here that, while Francis was praying, a voice came to him from the wood of the cross and said: 'Francis, go and repair my house, which as you see is in utter ruins.'[6] In this little place the virgin Clare shut herself up for love of her heavenly spouse. Here, hiding from the clamour of the world, she immured her body for the rest of her life. In the hollow of this wall, like the silver dove building her nest,[7] she founded her company of virgins of Christ, established a holy monastery, and began the Order of Poor Ladies.[8] Here, on her path of penance, she wore out the clay of her earthly members,[9] here she sowed the seeds of perfect justice; here by her own life

she showed the way to those who were to follow in her footsteps. In this narrow confinement for 42 years she broke the alabaster of her body with the severity of her discipline, so that the house of the Church might be suffused with the odour of her sanctity.[10] The true glory of her life in this place will become plain if first an account is given of how many and how great were the souls who came to Christ through her.

How Her Reputation for Holiness Spread Far and Wide

In a short while Clare's reputation for holiness spread through the neighbouring regions and women were drawn from all sides[11] to savour the odour of her sanctity. Virgins hastened to follow her example and preserve their virginity for Christ; married women strove to live their lives more chastely; women of rank and distinction turned their backs on spacious palaces[12] and built austere little convents for themselves and thought it a great glory to live for Christ in sackcloth and ashes. Young men, too, were equally inspired to join the struggle for purity, and were spurred to disdain the temptations of the flesh by the bold example of the weaker sex. Finally, many who were already joined in marriage bound themselves by mutual consent to the law of continence: the men entered monastic orders, the women the convents.[13] Mothers called daughters to Christ, and daughters their mothers; sister induced sister, aunts their nieces. Everyone rivalled each other in their fervour to serve Christ; everyone wanted to become a participant in this angelic life of which Clare was such a shining example. Countless virgins, moved by tales of Clare, but not being able to embrace the life of the cloister, strove to live the religious life without a Rule in their own homes. So many were these seeds of salvation that the virgin Clare brought forth that in her the prophecy was seen to be fulfilled: 'More are the children of the barren woman than the children of her who has a husband.'[14]

1 Many girls went into monasteries, but Clare's relatives thought her behaviour was beneath one of her gentility. She had sold her dowry and given it to the poor, and at San Paolo she would have been no better than a servant.

2 Clare's resistance underlines her great strength of character. She was on her own: Francis, it seems, did not intervene, and the monastery does not seem to have asserted its rights of sanctuary.

3 Sant' Angelo in (or di) Panzo was a church on the slopes of Monte Subasio with a small, informal community of women religious living nearby. Perhaps Clare thought she could live closer to her ideal of extreme poverty there than at San Paolo.

4 The small church of St Damian's (San Damiano), about half a mile south of Assisi, is of central importance to the early history of the Franciscan movement. Francis had restored it when it was in ruins.

5 See Thomas of Celano's *First Life* of St Francis, chapter 9.

6 The ancient crucifix which spoke to him is now in St George's Chapel in the Basilica of St Clare in Assisi.

7 Compare Song of Solomon 2.14.

8 At least some of the sisters of San Damiano were indeed noblewomen, and their title is reminiscent of tales of chivalry and knightly romance. Clare is regularly referred to as 'the Lady Clare'. According to St Bonaventure (*c.* 1217–74) the sisters were originally known as the 'Poor Ladies of Saints Cosmas and Damian', but after St Clare's canonization, they were called the 'Sisters of St Clare'. In the papal letters they are styled 'poor nuns' or 'poor enclosed Damianites'. An amusing, and unlikely, account of how they acquired their name is recorded in *New Fioretti* (*Omnibus* 1849f.). While restoring St Damian's, Francis made a famous prophecy concerning the future community of women who would come there (Celano, *Second Life*, chapter 24).

9 Literally she 'trampled on the soil [clods of earth] of her members'.

10 Literally 'the fragrance of her ointments'. (See above on chapter 4, n. 8.) Here Clare's 'fragrance' clearly refers to her spiritual blessings, the supernatural graces which manifest themselves in saints. There is an allusion here to Mary's pound of spikenard at John 12.3.

11 The sisters at St Damian's were by no means all locals: several came from further afield. One of the witnesses at the Process came from Rome.

12 Perhaps the most famous of these was Agnes of Prague, with whom Clare corresponded. According to one contemporary historian, Agnes was to have married the Emperor Frederick II (see Letter I), but turned her back on the world and founded a monastery of Clares in Prague in 1236.

13 See *Rule*, chapter II, note 3.

14 Compare Isaiah 54.1; also Galatians 4.27, where Paul applies the image to Mother Church, the new Jerusalem.

How Talk of Her Goodness Reached Even Distant Parts

11 Meanwhile, so that this source of heavenly blessing which had sprung up in the valley of Spoleto should not be hemmed within narrow confines, by the dispensation of divine providence it grew into a great river, so that the streams thereof might make glad the whole city of the Church.[1] For the sensation caused by these events spread far and wide in the world and everywhere began to win souls for Christ. Clare remained enclosed, but she began to enlighten the whole world, and won dazzling renown through the praises heaped upon her.[2] The fame of her virtues filled the chambers of noble ladies, it reached the palaces of duchesses, and found its way even into the private apartments of queens. The highest of the nobility stooped to follow in her footsteps, forgot its proud lineage and abased itself in holy humility. Some worthy of marriage to dukes and kings answered Clare's call and did severe penance, and those already married to powerful men followed Clare's example as best they could.[3] Countless cities were beautified with monasteries, and even the plains and mountains of the countryside were graced with the buildings of this celestial Order.[4] Under the most holy leadership of Clare, the cult of chastity became widespread in the world, and the ideal of virginity was revived and restored to its former honour. With these rich blossoms brought forth by Clare

the Church is decked today, and with them, too, she asks to be supported. 'Stay me with flowers,' she says; 'encompass me with apples, for I am sick with love.'[5]

But I must now return to my theme and describe Clare's way of life.

NOTES

1 Compare Psalm 46.4.
2 Again the play on Clare and 'light': *Clara . . . clarescere . . . praeclara refulget*.
3 Agnes of Prague has already been mentioned. Add St Elizabeth of Hungary (d. 1231), who after her husband's, death became a Tertiary; and Blessed Salomea of Krakow (*c.* 1219–68), originally a Tertiary, who founded the convent of Poor Clares at Zawichost; and Blessed Cunegund (Kinga) Queen of Poland (1224–92), niece of St Elizabeth of Hungary, who died a Tertiary in the convent she founded at Sandez.
4 During Clare's lifetime many houses of Poor Sisters sprang up all over Italy and much of Europe. John Moorman (*A History of the Franciscan Order from Its Origins to the Year 1517* (1968) p. 39) quotes a document of 1228 which gives the names of 23 houses in Italy. Elsewhere the same author numbers 147 houses founded before Clare's death in 1253.
5 Compare Song of Solomon 2.5.

—

Her Holy Humility

—

12 Clare, the cornerstone and noble foundation of her Order, strove from the very beginning to build an edifice of all virtues on the foundation of humility.[1] For she promised holy obedience to blessed Francis and never strayed from her promise. Three years after her conversion she declined the name and office of abbess and in her humility preferred to be subject to others rather than to be set above them, and was more willing to serve among the handmaids of Christ than to be served.[2] But when blessed Francis insisted, she finally undertook the supervision of the Ladies – an office which brought her anxiety rather than pride, and which increased not her freedom, but her servitude.

Clare washes the sisters' feet

For the more highly she was regarded in this position of authority, the more lowly she thought herself, the more ready to serve she was, and the less worthy of deference in her own eyes. She never shrank from any menial tasks, indeed she often washed the sisters' hands, served them at table, and waited on them as they ate. She gave an order only with reluctance; she preferred to act on impulse, choosing rather to do something herself than tell the sisters to do it. She herself washed the stools[3] of the sick, she herself, with that noble spirit of hers, wiped them clean, neither shying from their filth, nor shrinking from their stench. Often she washed the feet of the serving sisters when they returned from outside the monastery, and when she had washed them pressed kisses upon them. Once she was washing the feet of a lay sister, and when she stooped to kiss them, the sister, unable to endure such a show of humility, withdrew her foot and as she did so struck Clare on the mouth. But Clare gently took the sister's foot in her hand and planted a firm kiss on its sole.[4]

NOTES

1 Humility was traditionally regarded as the cornerstone of all the virtues. Celano calls it the 'guardian and ornament of all virtues', and adds: 'If the spiritual building does not rest upon it, it will fall in ruins' (*Second Life*, chapter 140).

2 The moment was significant, marking the first stage in the development of the Poor Ladies as an enclosed order. 'Abbess' was a Benedictine title, and Benedictine abbesses enjoyed a great degree of autonomy. Clare may have refused the office because she was afraid it might change her community at St Damian's into something like that at San Paolo delle Abbadesse. Service is the key-word in Clare's concept of the duties of abbess.

3 The Latin word is *sedilia*. Regis Armstrong (*Clare: Early Documents*) takes it to mean the straw-filled palliasses on which the sisters slept. But the meaning of 'stools' (= seat used for the evacuation of the bowels, then 'faeces') is well attested, and probably correct here.

4 A fact independently attested by three of the sisters at the *Process*. Sister Agnes (daughter of the mayor of Assisi) once drank the water in which Clare had washed her feet and pronounced it 'sweet and delicious'. With typical good sense Clare threw the water away, as if to declare that she wanted nothing to do with penance so extreme. But such acts were not unheard of: Angelo of Foligno, a contemporary mystic (*c.* 1248–1309) kissed the water with which she had washed the putrefied limbs of a leper.

24

13 Her poverty in all material things went hand in hand[1] with poverty of spirit, which is true humility.[2] First of all, at the beginning of her conversion, she sold all her paternal inheritance[3] and, keeping none of the proceeds for herself, gave it all to the poor. Then, having left the world outside and enriched her mind within, she ran after Christ unencumbered by any earthly burdens.[4] So close, in fact, was the compact she made with holy poverty and so great her love for it that she wanted to possess nothing but the Lord Christ, and would not allow her sisters to possess anything. For she was convinced that the most precious pearl of heavenly desire, which she had sold all she had to purchase,[5] could never be possessed along with a gnawing care for worldly things. Frequently in her talks she impressed upon the sisters that their community would only be acceptable to God when it was rich in poverty, and that it would only remain stable for ever if it were always protected by the watchtower of the most sublime poverty. She exhorted them to model themselves in their little nest of poverty on the poor Christ, whom his poor mother lay as a baby in a narrow manger.[6] With this special remembrance Clare encircled her breast, as if with a necklace of gold, lest the dust of earthly things should enter her heart.

14 Wishing that her Order should be known as a poor Order, Clare asked Pope Innocent III, of happy memory,[7] for the Privilege of Poverty. This magnanimous prelate, expressing his delight at her great fervour, declared that her proposal was unique, since such a privilege had never been asked of the Apostolic See before. And wishing to accord this unusual request a favour equally unusual, the Pope with great joy wrote the first draft of the privilege she had asked for with his own hand.[8] The Lord Pope Gregory,[9] of happy memory – who was most worthy of the papal throne, as he was revered for his virtues – loved the saint as dearly as a father loves his own child. When he was trying to persuade her

that, because of the political situation and the dangers of the times, she should agree to have some possessions, which he himself freely offered her, Clare determinedly resisted him, and would not hear of such a thing. The Pope replied: 'If you are afraid of breaking your vow, we release you from it.' 'Holy father,' she said, 'I never wish to be released in any way from following Christ for ever.'[10]

When the questors[11] brought back scraps and morsels of bread, Clare accepted them most gladly, indeed she seemed almost sad when there were whole loaves, and was much happier with scraps. In a word, she strove by a most perfect poverty to make herself like the poor crucified Christ, so that nothing mortal should separate the lover from her beloved or hinder her progress towards the Lord.

Now here are two miracles which this lover of poverty was given grace to perform.

NOTES

1 Reading *concinebat* for *continebat*.

2 In his poem *Praises of the Virtues*, Francis talks of poverty and humility as sisters: in his mind the two were linked inextricably.

3 According to *Process* XII 3 she sold part of her younger sister Beatrice's inheritance too.

4 Compare Luke 10.4; 22.35.

5 Compare Matthew 13.44ff., and Celano *First Life*, chapter 6. Francis 'hid the pearl he had discovered . . . and in secret tried to sell all his possessions in order to buy it.'

6 Compare the fourth letter to Agnes of Prague. Clare is constantly visualizing the persons of Jesus and his Mother in terms of their poverty and helplessness.

7 Innocent III was pope from 1198 to 1216.

8 We possess what seems to be the original of this crucial document. Its authenticity was long doubted, but has now been accepted on the basis of three ancient manuscripts from Messina, Madrid and Uppsala. It is not clear if Innocent III granted oral or written approval of Clare's petition, but it is certain that Gregory IX did confirm it in writing in September 1228 (though subsequently he tried to mitigate some of its provisions). The Privilege of Poverty gives official recognition to the unique status of St Damian's. (A monastery without property was quite unheard of.)

9 Gregory IX (Hugolino) became pope in 1227.

10 Clare was daring: Gregory was pope, after all, and Protector of the Order and had been a close friend of Francis. But here, only two years after the saint's death, Clare is already fighting to defend his ideals.

11 Questors were the friars who begged alms for the sisters.

The Miracle of the Multiplication of Bread

15 There was only one loaf of bread in the monastery, and it was time for the sisters' meal and they were hungry. Calling the refectorian[1] Clare told her to divide the loaf and send half of it to the brothers, and to keep the rest for the sisters. She told her to break their half into fifty pieces, equalling the number of sisters,[2] and to place them before the sisters on their meagre table. When her devout daughter replied that they would need one of the ancient miracles of Christ if fifty portions were to be got from such a small piece of bread, her mother answered: 'My daughter, do not worry, just do as I say.' While the daughter made haste to carry out her mother's command, Clare made haste to voice her pious concerns for her daughters to her Christ. And by a gift from heaven, the little piece of bread increased in the hands of the sister who was breaking it and there was a generous portion for everyone in the community.[3]

NOTES

1 The refectorian (*dispensatrix*) is the sister in charge of catering.

2 Luke Wadding, the Franciscan historian (1588–1657), furnishes a list of the names of 51 sisters at St Damian's for the year 1238 (*Annales* 1238 XIV–XV t. III p. 13).

3 This miracle is attested by Sister Cecilia (*Process* VI 16).

Another Miracle: the Oil Given by God

—

16 One day the handmaids of Christ had so little oil left that they had none even to season the food for the sick. The Lady Clare picked up an oil jar and, mistress of humility as she was, washed it with her own hands, then set this empty jar aside so that the brother questor could take it with him when he went begging for alms. The brother was then called and asked to find them some oil. This devoted brother, anxious to relieve their pressing need at once, ran to fetch the jar. But 'it is not of him that willeth, nor of him that runneth, but of God that sheweth mercy'.[1] For through God's mediation, and his alone, the vessel was found full of oil, because St Clare's prayer had anticipated the brother's concern for the well-being of the poor daughters. But the brother in question, thinking he had been called out for nothing, muttered to himself: 'These women called me just to make fun of me. Look! The jar is full!'[2]

NOTES

1 Compare Romans 9.18.
2 This miracle is attested by two witnesses in the *Process* (I 15 and II 14).

—

Her Mortification of the Flesh

—

17 It would perhaps be better to remain silent rather than to speak of Clare's remarkable mortification[1] of her flesh, since she did things which it would astonish people to hear of, and which they would find hard to believe. It was not unusual for her to wear a simple tunic and a poor mantle of rough cloth, merely covering her little body rather than keeping it warm. And we should not be surprised that she disdained the use of shoes. It was nothing unusual for her to fast all year round, or to sleep on a bed without a mattress. These are things for which perhaps she does not merit any particular praise, since there were other sisters in her monastery who did the same. But what was a young lady doing wearing pigskin next to her flesh? For this most holy virgin had got herself a garment made from the roughly shorn skin of a pig, which she secretly wore under her tunic with the sharp bristles against her flesh.[2] Sometimes she would wear a coarse shirt made of knotted horsehair which she tied to her body with rough cords. One day she acceded to the request of one of her daughters and lent this garment to her, but after three days of wearing it this sister could not stand the discomfort and she was even more eager to give it up than she had been to borrow it. The bare ground, or sometimes some vine branches, served as her bed, and a hard block of wood served her as a pillow. In the course of time, when her body became weak, she slept on a rush mat and allowed her head the indulgence of a bit of straw. And when after many years of harsh treatment her body finally succumbed to a long illness, at the command of blessed Francis she used a sack filled with straw.[3]

18 So rigorous, too, was her abstinence in fasting that she could scarcely have kept herself alive on the small amounts she ate, were it not for some other strength that sustained her.[4] For while she still enjoyed good health she fasted on bread and water during the Greater Lent and the Lent of St Martin the Bishop,[5] and tasted wine, if there were any, only on Sundays. And, though those incapable of such rigours may find it hard to believe, on three days of the week during the two Lents, that is on Mondays, Wednesdays and Fridays, Clare ate nothing at all. So days of meagre refreshment and days of utter mortification followed one after the other, so that a vigil of complete fasting was relieved as it were by a feast of bread and water. It is hardly surprising that such rigours, observed for such a long time, made her subject to illnesses, consumed her strength, and sapped her bodily

energy. Her most devoted daughters saw this and suffered with their holy mother, and they tearfully bemoaned the mortifications she underwent so willingly each day. At length Francis and the Bishop of Assisi forbade the saintly Clare to keep her dangerous three-days fast and told her she must never let a day pass without eating at least an ounce and a half of bread.[6] Although severe affliction of the body generally causes affliction of the spirit, Clare, on the contrary, was utterly radiant. During all her mortifications she kept a bright and cheerful expression on her face, seeming either not to feel her bodily discomforts or to be laughing at them. From this it can be seen quite clearly that the mystical joy with which she was inwardly flooded was overflowing outwardly. For the heart's love makes light of bodily affliction.

NOTES

1 The word 'mortification' occurs rarely in Franciscan texts, but is used four times in the *Legend* alone. Perhaps this is indicative of an increasingly penitential movement in thirteenth-century spirituality.

2 Sister Benvenuta (*Process* II 7) tells us that the sisters took this garment away from Clare when she was ill.

3 This was not the only time Francis had to intervene in order to relax Clare's austerities (see chapter 18).

4 Traditionally, fasting meant eating only one meal a day of cereals, vegetable and fruit, preferably raw and without vegetable fats. During Lent meats and animal fats were not allowed. So breaking a fast meant either eating more than one meal a day, or eating prohibited foods (which Francis permitted on Sundays and at Christmas). Sister Amata (*Process* IV 5) states that the portions of food consumed by Clare were 'so tiny it seemed she was fed by angels'.

5 The Greater Lent lasted from Ash Wednesday to Easter Day; the Lesser Lent, or St Martin's Lent, generally from 11 November to Christmas. St Martin (d. 397) was Bishop of Tours.

6 Francis' advice had perhaps not been heeded by Clare, so he had sought the support of Bishop Guido. Clare, who was always lenient with others, finally learnt to be easier on herself. In her third letter to Agnes, she begs her to abandon her excessive rigours in fasting.

Of Her Practice of Holy Prayer

19 Clare, being truly dead to the flesh and completely estranged from the world, occupied her soul continually with holy prayers[1] and divine praises. She had already fixed the most fervent gaze of her inward desire upon the light, and having soared far above all earthly confusions was now unfolding the depths of her soul ever more widely to showers of graces. She prayed with the sisters for long hours after Compline,[2] and as floods of tears broke from her eyes,[3] others too were moved to weep. And after the rest went to refresh their tired bodies in their hard beds, Clare would remain in prayer, indomitably vigilant, hoping that when sleep had overtaken the others, she might catch in secret the faintest whisper from heaven.[4] Very often, when she was lying prostrate on her face in prayer, she would wet the ground with her tears and caress it with her kisses, so that she seemed always to be clasping her Jesus in her arms, her tears flowing over his feet and her kisses imprinted on them.[5] Once, as at dead of night she was weeping, an angel of darkness appeared at her side in the form of a little black boy, and uttered the warning: 'Do not weep so much or you will become blind.'[6] Clare at once retorted: 'No-one that sees God shall be blind.' And the demon departed in confusion. The same night after Matins[7] as Clare was praying and bathed as usual in a flood of tears, the treacherous counsellor came to her again. 'Do not weep so much,' he said, 'or in the end your brain will go soft and stream through your nostrils, and you will end up with a crooked nose!'[8] Clare swiftly replied: 'No-one who serves the Lord suffers any such torment.'[9] And at once the demon slipped away and disappeared.

20 How much strength she received in the furnace of her fervent prayer, and the bliss God's goodness granted her in its enjoyment, was evident from the usual signs. For when she rejoined the sisters in joy after holy prayer, she brought from the fire of the altar of the Lord burning words, words which set

the hearts of the sisters aflame. Indeed they were astonished at the sweetness which issued from her lips and the way her face shone more brightly than usual.[10] For truly God in his sweetness had provided for his poor one[11] and was showing outwardly in her body the true light which had filled her soul in prayer. Thus, in a perishable world, imperishably wed to her noble spouse, Clare took continual delight in the things above. Thus, sustained by steadfast virtue on the ever-moving wheel of worldly fortune, and enclosing the treasure of glory in a vessel of clay,[12] Clare's body remained below, but her soul remained on high. It was her custom to go to Matins before the younger sisters, and she would wake them quietly with a touch[13] and call them to worship. She would often light the lamps while the the rest were sleeping; often too she would ring the bell with her own hand. In her community there was no place for lukewarmness or idleness: any laziness in prayer or in the service of the Lord would be corrected by a sharp rebuke.

NOTES

1 Clare's devotion to prayer, and the power she derived from it, are the focal point of the next third of the *Legend*.

2 Compline is the last of the canonical day-hours, said before retiring.

3 Many saints have been given the gift of tears during prayer and meditation. St Aelred of Rievaulx called tears 'the signs of perfect prayer'. Among others, St Elizabeth of Hungary frequently wept copiously at prayer or after her visions, and according to *The Golden Legend*, St Peter wept so often that his whole face 'seemed to be wasted with weeping'.

4 The Vulgate has the same phrase at Job 4.12.

5 That is, she became so immersed in her prayer that she re-enacted the scene she so vividly visualized – that of Mary Magdalene covering Jesus' feet with kisses.

6 A curious episode, but the devil has traditionally made the most disgusting suggestions to saints, based on their fears of one kind or another. Marie d'Oignies, for example, was similarly tempted, as was St Teresa of Avila. St Francis, of course, did go blind, and this was thought to be because of his excessive weeping.

7 Matins, until the eleventh century called Vigils, was the first canonical hour, and originally performed at midnight, but the Rule of St Benedict

dictated that it take place at 2.00 a.m. Clare's Rule does not specify the hours for offices, but Sister Benvenuta (*Process* III 9) tells us that Clare woke the sisters around midnight for Matins.

8 Text: I follow the reading of the Acta Sanctorum: *emunxeris* for *emunxerit*.

9 The devil has said that Clare's nose will be crooked, or twisted (*tortum*). Clare replies that no-one who serves the Lord suffers 'torment' ('twisting', 'torture', from Latin *torqueo*). The devil seems to be saying that Clare will need to wipe her nose so often that it will go crooked.

10 The radiance of Clare's face is corroborated by at least three of her sisters, and indeed another sister (*Process* II 7) swears that even her place of prayer shone. Similar phenomena are recorded for e.g. St Clare of Montefalco and St Catherine of Siena.

11 Compare Psalm 68.10.

12 Compare 2 Corinthians 4.7.

13 The Latin says 'by signs'. Sister Agnes (*Process* X 3) tells us that Clare woke them by touching them in silence.

The Miracles Worked by Her Prayers
First: The Saracens Miraculously Put to Flight

21 At this point I propose to relate some of the miracles worked by her prayers, miracles as well attested as they are worthy of all veneration.

During the tribulations that the Church had to suffer in various parts of the world under the Emperor Frederick,[1] the valley of Spoleto had to drink all too often from the chalice of wrath.[2] For bands of soldiers and Saracen archers, swarming like so many bees, were posted there at the Emperor's command to lay waste its towns and storm its cities. And when on one occasion the fury of the enemy was turned upon Assisi, God's special city, and an army was approaching its very gates, the Saracens,[3] that most evil race, who thirst after the blood of Christians and recklessly commit every kind of wickedness, poured into the precincts of St Damian's and entered even the enclosure of the virgins. The poor ladies fainted away with fright, their voices trembled with terror,

33

and they ran in tears to their mother. Clare was undismayed: though she was sick, she told them to take her to the door[4] and set her in the path of the enemy, carrying before her the silver casket enclosed in ivory in which the body of the Most Holy One was most devoutly kept.[5]

22 She then prostrated herself fully in prayer to the Lord, and with tears in her eyes said to her Christ: 'Is it your wish, Lord, to give these defenceless handmaids of yours, whom I have nurtured with your love, into the hands of pagans such as these? Defend, O Lord, I beseech you, your servants whom at this time I am unable to defend.' Suddenly from the mercy seat of his special grace a voice like that of a small child sounded in her ears. 'I will always defend you.' 'My Lord,' she said, 'if you will, protect this city too, which supports us for love of you.'[6] And Christ replied: 'It will suffer hardships, but under my protection it will be kept safe.' Then Clare, raising her tearful face, comforted her weeping sisters. 'My daughters,' she said, 'I give you my word that you will suffer no harm. Only trust in Christ.' And in a moment the insolence of the Saracen dogs was checked and turned to fear. Quickly they climbed back over the walls they had scaled, utterly vanquished by the power of the virgin's prayer. And Clare immediately called those of the sisters who had heard the child's voice and gave them a solemn warning. 'My dearest daughters, be sure never to breathe a word about that voice to anyone so long as I live.'[7]

NOTES

1 Emperor Frederick II, in 1240 excommunicated for the second time, was attempting to gain control of the whole peninsula. Instead of going on his promised crusade to the Holy Land, Frederick was using Saracens in a private 'crusade' in Italy, sacking those cities of Umbria that, like Assisi, supported the pope.

2 Compare Revelation 14.10.

3 The assault can be pinpointed to September 1240. These 'Saracens' were Moslem mercenaries in the Emperor's pay. Saracens had once dominated

34

the deep south of Italy and Sicily, and there are numerous survivals of their language in place-names and dialect.

4 Traditionally Clare made her appearance at the first floor (west) window of the monastery dormitory, where the Saracens were trying to force an entrance.

5 Clare is often depicted holding aloft a monstrance (not a pyx, as described here). This may reflect her intense devotion to the blessed Sacrament, a devotion which became prevalent generally in the thirteenth century. In art the Saracens are blinded by the dazzling light issuing from the monstrance: the blind pagans are repelled by the radiant body of Christ.

6 Clare is presented as the patroness and defender of her city: her bond with Assisi is thus established and official.

7 Her solemn warning (reminiscent of Jesus' frequent instructions to those he has healed not to tell anyone) was probably motivated partly by her humility, but also partly by the fear that talk of 'miracles' would inevitably attract unwanted attention, and encourage the growth of an unofficial *cultus*. (Compare chapter 31 (end).)

Another Miracle: the Liberation of the City

23 On another occasion[1] the captain of the imperial army, Vitalis d'Aversa, a man eager for glory and valiant in battle, led his troops against Assisi. He stripped the land of its trees, laid waste all the surrounding countryside, and positioned himself to besiege the city, swearing in menacing tones that he would never withdraw until he had taken it. Things had reached such a pass that there were fears that the city might be lost any moment. When Clare, the servant of Christ, heard this, she groaned aloud, and, calling the sisters to her, said: 'My dearest daughters, we receive many good things every day from this city. We would be failing in our duty if we did not do all we can to help it in its hour of need.' She then had some ashes fetched and told the sisters to uncover their heads. First she bared her own head and poured handful after handful of ashes over it; then she did the same on the heads of the sisters. 'Go and pray to our Lord,' she told them, 'and beg him with all your heart to save the city.'

35

The liberation of Assisi. The imperial army is repelled

What need to dwell on details, to describe the virgins' tears, or their frenzied prayers? Next morning God in his mercy brought their trial to a happy conclusion:[2] the whole army was scattered and its proud commander, despite the oath he had sworn, went away and never harassed the land again. In fact not long after this he himself perished by the sword.

1 This incident, like the former, is amply attested in the *Process* and can be dated to the summer of 1241. Assisi's deliverance is commemorated annually on 22 June with the *Festa del Voto*. The cult of Clare became a symbol of the unity of the whole city.
2 Compare 1 Corinthians 10.13.

The Power of Her Prayer in the Conversion of Her Sister

24 But we must not pass over in silence the miraculous power of her prayer by which, at the very beginning of her own conversion, Clare converted another soul to God, then kept her convert safe. For she had a sister of tender age, a sister of the same blood and same purity of life. Clare longed for her conversion, and among the first-fruits of the prayers she offered to God with all her heart, she begged most earnestly that, just as she had been united in spirit with her sister in the world, so they should now be united in will in the service of God. So she prayed insistently to the Father of Mercy that Agnes,[1] the sister she had left at home, should weary of the world's staleness and taste the sweeetness of God, and that he should turn her from any thoughts of an earthly marriage to the union of his love, so that together with her in perpetual virginity she might be wedded to the Spouse of Glory. Though these two sisters were of different temperaments, the love they shared was extraordinarily deep, and it had made the recent separation painful for both. The Divine Majesty swiftly gave ear to this noble suppliant, and speedily granted her this first gift that she so insistently craved and that so delighted God to give. For, sixteen days[2] after the conversion of Clare, Agnes was inspired by the Holy Spirit to hasten to join her sister; she explained to her her secret desire, and told her that she wished to devote herself wholly to the service of God. Embracing her

joyfully, Clare said: 'I give thanks to God, my sweetest sister, that he has heard my anxious prayers for you.'

25 After this remarkable conversion Clare safeguarded her sister in a way that was equally remarkable. While the sisters were happily following in the footsteps of Christ at the Church of Sant'Angelo in Panzo and Clare, who knew more of the Lord, was instructing her novice sister, the relatives of the two girls suddenly began to make new trouble for them. When they heard that Agnes had gone to join Clare, twelve of her male relatives, hot with anger, ran to the place and, concealing their evil purpose, pretended that they had come in peace. Immediately they rounded on Agnes (for they had long ago despaired of Clare) and said: 'Why have you come to this place? Come back home with us now and be quick about it.' And when Agnes replied that she would not leave her sister Clare, one of the men, a knight, went wild: he rushed at her, punching and kicking her, and attempted to drag her away by the hair, while the rest pushed her from behind and then tried to lift her off her feet. At this the young Agnes, as if she had been seized by lions and was being torn from the hands of the Lord, cried out: 'Help me, dearest sister! Do not let me be taken from Christ the Lord!' Then, while her cruel abductors were dragging the young girl down the mountainside, despite all her resistance, tearing her clothing and strewing the path with the hair they had torn from her head, Clare tearfully prostrated herself in prayer and asked that her sister should be given the willpower to endure this, and that the enemy's fury might be overcome by power from on high.

26 Suddenly, as Agnes lay there on the ground, her body seemed so heavy, so absolutely rooted there that, though several of them strove with all their might, the men were unable to carry her beyond a little stream. Other men, too, came running from the fields and the vineyards and did their utmost to help them, but they were utterly powerless to lift her body from the ground. And when, despite all their efforts, they had finally to admit defeat, they tried to play down the miracle with the sneer: 'She has been eating lead all night: no wonder she is so heavy!' Now her uncle, Lord Monaldo,[3] was so enraged that he would have dealt her a fatal blow, but the hand he raised was suddenly racked with a terrible pain, and this pain continued to torment him cruelly for some time afterwards. Then all at once, after Agnes' long struggle, Clare appeared on the scene and asked her relatives to stop their hostility and to entrust Agnes (who was lying there half dead) to her safekeeping. Bitter at the failure of their mission they withdrew, and at once Agnes got up happily and, rejoicing in the cross of Christ for whom she had fought this first battle, gave herself for ever to the service of God. Blessed Francis cut off her hair with his own hands[4] and together with her sister instructed her in the way of the Lord. But since it would be impossible to explain in a few words the great perfection of Agnes' life,[5] let us concentrate on Clare.

NOTES

1 Agnes was born *c.* 1197–8 and was about 15 when she followed Clare into religion. Her baptismal name was probably Caterina, and Agnes the name she took in religion. Clare had at least one other sister, Beatrice, who was youngest of all.

2 This dates the flight of Agnes to 2 April 1212. Agnes joined Clare at Sant' Angelo di Panzo where she was staying before her removal to St Damian's.

3 Monaldo apparently was the head of the family, and older than Clare's father.

4 So repeating the extraordinary gesture made earlier to Clare.

5 Agnes became first abbess of the monastery at Monticelli, Florence, and opened other houses at Padua, Venice and Mantua. She returned to St Damian's in 1253 where she died three months after her sister. She was first buried at St Damian's, then her body was moved to lie alongside that of her sister in the new church of Santa Chiara in Assisi. Her tomb was celebrated for miracles, and her *cultus* was confirmed by Pope Benedict XIV. Her feast day is kept on 16 November.

Another Miracle: the Exorcism of Demons

27 If the prayers of Clare prevailed against the wickedness of men, it is not surprising that they also consumed demons. There was a devout woman of the diocese of Pisa who once came to the monastery to give thanks to God and St Clare because through the merits of the saint she had been freed from five demons. In fact the demons said when they were cast out that it was the prayers of St Clare that were torturing them and forcing them to leave the body of the woman possessed.

The Lord Pope Gregory had a remarkable faith in the prayers of this saint, and not without reason, for he had seen their power in action. Often indeed when some new difficulty arose, as they will, both when he was Bishop of Ostia and when later he had been raised to the Apostolic See, he wrote to Clare asking for her prayers,[1] and benefited from her help. That the Vicar of Christ should seek help from a handmaid of Christ and commend himself to her prayers is surely something which is both admirable for its humility and worthy of the most zealous imitation. He well knew what love can do, and how freely pure virgins are granted access to the Throne of Majesty. For if the King of Heaven gives himself to those who love him fervently, what is there, if it be fitting, that he will not grant them when they ask for it in faith?

NOTES

1 Two letters survive. (See *Early Documents* 101–4.) This one was written in 1220 after a visit by Hugolino to St Damian's for Holy Week. The second was written after his election as pope, and before the canonization of St Francis. They are brief but interesting indications of the character of the prelate and his relationship with Clare.

Clare casts five demons from a woman of Pisa

Her Wonderful Devotion to the
Sacrament of the Altar

28 The depth of St Clare's devotion to the Sacrament of the
Altar[1] is clearly shown by the fact that when she was
bed-ridden during her grave illness, she had herself lifted upright
and propped up on cushions and, sitting there in her bed, she

spun the finest cloth. From it she made more than fifty sets of corporals,[2] enclosed them in burses of silk or purple cloth and sent them to various churches over the plains and mountains of Assisi.

When she was about to receive the body of the Lord, she first wept burning tears; then approached in trembling,[3] for she feared her Saviour no less hidden in the sacrament than ruling over heaven and earth.

NOTES

1 The mystery of the Eucharist had a place of overriding importance in Clare's life, as it had in Francis'. (See Angela of Foligno, *The Divine Consolations* XXXIX, on the central place of the Eucharist in the life of the aspiring Christian.) Attention had turned away from Crusades and the Holy Sepulchre, and the new religious houses of women served to spread the popularity of this devotion. The Fourth Lateran Council had prescribed that communion must be taken at least once a year. According to Clare (*Rule* chapter III) the sisters were required to make their communion a minimum of seven times a year. Clare herself may have done so more often, though her enclosure and dependence on a visiting chaplain may in practice have limited the possibilities.

2 Clare (who is the patroness of embroidery) spun and wove, which is skilful and painstaking work. A beautiful linen alb she made for St Francis is still preserved by the Clares in Assisi. According to witnesses in the *Process* she made burses lined with silk or precious cloth to hold the corporals, had them blessed by Bishop Guido and delivered to all the local churches.

3 Angela of Foligno in the *Divine Consolations* (late 1200s) uses much the same language: 'We should therefore approach that table . . . with the utmost reverence, fear and trembling.'

———

A Truly Wonderful Consolation that the Lord Granted Her in Her Illness

———

29 Just as Clare was always mindful[1] of Christ in her illness, so too Christ visited her in her sufferings.[2] At that hour of the Nativity when the world shouts for joy with the angels at the birth of the little child, all the Ladies went to the oratory for Matins, and left their mother alone, burdened as she was with her

afflictions. And when she began to think about the little Jesus, and was lamenting the fact that she could not share in his praises, she said with a sigh: 'Lord God, look at me, left all on my own in this place.' No sooner had she spoken than the wonderful music that was being made in the church of St Francis began to ring in her ears. She heard the joyful voices of the friars chanting the psalms,[3] she could make out the harmonies of the singers, she even caught the sounds of the instruments playing.[4] Now the church of St Francis was much too far away[5] for the sound to have been heard by any human ear: it must have been that the music of the solemnity was magnified and carried to her by the will of heaven, or that her hearing was endowed with more than human power.[6] But what surpassed even this, was that she was given grace to see the very manger of the Lord.[7] Next morning, when her daughters came to see her Clare said: 'Blessed be the Lord Jesus Christ, for though you left me, he would not leave me. Truly, by the grace of Christ, I heard all the solemnities which were celebrated last night in the church of St Francis.'[8]

NOTES

1 The Latin (*memoria memor erat*) is reminiscent of Lamentations 3.20 (Vulgate).

2 Clare was ill for at least 28 years, i.e. from 1224–5 until her death.

3 For a special occasion, the monks probably sang the psalms in the traditional plainchant tones, and may also have performed some responsaries in harmony.

4 The Latin *organorum* could mean 'organs', and so it is widely translated here. There may have been an organ in what was by now a patriarchal and papal basilica, but the word should probably be taken in a general sense, meaning 'musical instruments'.

5 St Damian's is about half a mile as the crow flies from the church of St Francis.

6 It was this celebrated example of clairaudience, traditionally dated 1252 (as well as the prophecy to Ortolana that Clare would be a light to illumine the world), that in 1958 prompted Pius XII to designate Clare as universal patroness of television.

7 An interesting detail, corroborated by Sister Amata (*Process* IV 16), which may indicate that the friars maintained the tradition Francis began at

Greccio at Christmas 1223 of creating a crib. Or else it could mean that Clare saw a vision of the actual crib at Bethlehem. She was greatly given to visualizing the young Christ-child.

8 In the expanded version of this story in the later *Little Flowers* (chapter 35), Clare is miraculously transported to the church to attend Matins and Mass of Midnight, then taken back to her bed. 'And moreover . . .,' she adds, 'I received Holy Communion there.'

—————

Her Most Fervent Love of the Crucified

30 Clare wept habitually over the Lord's Passion: at times deriving from his sacred wounds feelings as bitter as myrrh, at times sipping[1] joys that were sweeter. The tears of the suffering Christ utterly inebriated her, and she often pictured in her mind him whom love had imprinted so deeply on her heart.[2] She taught her novices to lament the crucified Christ, and what she taught them by word of mouth she daily demonstrated in practice. For often when she was about to exhort them in private about such things, her cheeks were wet with tears before she could utter a word. During the Hours of the day, at Sext and None[3] she habitually felt a greater compunction:[4] it was as if she were being immolated with her immolated Lord. And once when she was praying at the Hour of None in her tiny cell, the devil struck her on the jaw, gave her a bloodshot eye and bruised her cheek. And in order to feed her mind on the delights of the Crucified without interruption, she would very often meditate on the Prayer of the Five Wounds of the Lord.[5] She learnt the Office of the Cross,[6] as Francis, himself a lover of the cross, had composed it, and recited it often with as much feeling as he did. Beneath her habit she tied to her bare flesh a slender cord with thirteen knots as a secret memorial of the Saviour's wounds.

NOTES

1 Reading *sugit* for *fugit*.
2 For the importance of the crucifix to Clare see the letters to Agnes of Prague, especially I, II and IV.

3 Sext and None, the fourth and fifth canonical Hours, were at midday and 3.00 p.m.

4 Compunction is an important concept. In medieval times the word conveyed a more positive idea than it does today, that of a stinging (Latin *compungere*) reminder of God's presence, a stimulus to rise above one's sins.

5 The Prayer of the Five Wounds of the Lord (reproduced in *Early Documents*, p. 170, note a) concentrates on the physical agony of Jesus and is an aid to sharing in his sufferings. Its author is unknown.

6 Francis composed an Office of the Cross (see *Omnibus* pp. 141–55) which illustrates his own intense devotion to the crucified Christ. In it he tries to imagine the state of mind of the suffering Christ at the various stages of his passion.

Her Remembrance One Easter of
the Lord's Passion

31 One year the day of the most holy Supper[1] had arrived, when the Lord showed the final perfection of his love for his disciples.[2] Towards evening, as the hour of the Lord's agony was approaching, Clare, overcome with grief and sorrow, shut herself up in the seclusion of her cell. There in her prayer, as she followed the Lord himself in prayer and drained with him his cup of sadness, her soul was sorrowful even unto death,[3] and she became so transported as she remembered how he was taken and mocked that she fell upon her bed. All that night and the following day she remained so rapt and so lost to herself that her gaze was unblinking, her eyes were always intent upon one object, she seemed united with Christ and to be otherwise utterly insensible. A sister who was close to her visited her regularly to see if she wanted anything, and found her always in the same attitude. But when the eve of the Sabbath came,[4] this devout daughter lit a candle and took it to Clare, and without speaking gestured to her to remind her of St Francis' instruction. For the saint had forbidden her to let a day pass without eating.[5] Then as the sister stood beside her Clare came to herself again, as if returning from

another world, and asked: 'What need is there of a candle? Is it not daytime?' 'Mother,' replied the sister, 'the night has gone and a day has passed, and another night has come.' 'My dearest daughter,' said Clare, 'God be praised for the sleep I have had. I have desired it for so long, and at last it has been given to me. But be sure you never tell a soul about it so long as I live.'[6]

NOTES

1 Maundy Thursday.
2 Compare John 13.1.
3 Compare Matthew 26.38; Mark 14.34.
4 That is, Friday night, the next evening.
5 See above on chapter 18 and note 6.
6 Again, after a miracle/vision, Clare swears the witness to secrecy.

Various Miracles She Performed by the Sign and Power of the Cross

32 The Crucified One, so beloved of Clare as he was, repaid[1] her with an equal love, and because of the great love with which she burned for the mystery of the cross, she was exalted by the power of the cross to perform wonders and miracles. For whenever she made the sign of the life-giving cross over the sick, their diseases immediately disappeared. I will touch on one or two of many such instances.[2]

Blessed Francis, knowing of Clare's perfect holiness and respecting her great powers, sent to her a certain brother called Stephen, who was out of his mind, so that she might make the sign of the most holy cross over him. Obedient daughter that she was, Clare made the sign over him, as her father had asked her to, and let him sleep a while in the place where she was accustomed to pray. When he got up after a short sleep he was completely sane, and returned to Francis cured of his insanity.

33 A young boy of three[3] named Mattiolo, from the city of Spoleto, had a stone stuck in his nose. No-one could remove it, and the boy himself could not dislodge it by force. He was in great pain and seemed likely to die, but was taken to the Lady Clare, and when she made the sign of the cross over him the stone at once shot out of his nose and he was cured.

Another boy from Perugia was brought to the holy servant of God with one eye completely closed with an infection. Clare touched the boy's eye and made the sign of the cross on it and said: 'Take him to my mother for her to make a second sign of the cross upon him.' (Her mother, in fact, the Lady Ortolana, had followed her 'little plant' and entered the Order after her daughter, and, as a widow, was serving the Lord among the virgins in the enclosed garden.)[4] As soon as the boy had had the sign of the cross made over him, the disease cleared from his eye, and he could see with crystal clarity. So Clare maintained that the boy had been cured by the merit of her mother; but Ortolana refused to accept the credit, insisted that all the praise belonged to her daughter, and declared herself to be unworthy of such a miracle.

34 One of the sisters, named Benvenuta,[5] had been suffering for some 12 years with an ulcerous infection under her arm which discharged pus in five different places. The holy virgin Clare, moved by compassion for her, applied her special salve, the life-giving sign of the cross. And as soon as the sister received it, the wound she had nursed so long was gone and she was perfectly well again.

Another of the sisters, Amata,[6] had been suffering from dropsy for 13 months. She was racked by a fever, bouts of coughing, and a pain in her side as well, and was confined to her sick-bed. Out of pity for her the Lady Clare had recourse to the aid of her sovereign remedy. She made the sign of the cross on her in the name of her Christ, and at once restored her to perfect health.

35 Another handmaid of Christ, a native of Perugia,[7] had lost her voice for two years so completely that she could scarcely make a sound. On the night of the Assumption of Our Lady, it was revealed to her that the Lady Clare would cure her, and she could hardly wait for the daylight to come. As soon as it dawned, she hurried to her mother and asked her to make the sign of the cross over her, and no sooner had she done so than she recovered her voice.

A sister named Cristiana[8] had for a long time been deaf in one ear, and had taken many different medicines to cure it, but to no avail. Moved to pity the Lady Clare made the sign of the cross on her forehead, touched her ear, and she immediately recovered her power of hearing.

When there was a great number of sick sisters in the monastery, all suffering from different complaints, Clare went to the infirmary[9] with her customary medicine, and making the sign of the cross five times at once cured five of the sisters of their illnesses.[10]

From this it is abundantly clear that the tree of the cross had taken root in the bosom of the virgin Clare, and while its fruit refreshes the soul, its leaves provide medicine for the body.[11]

NOTES

1 Reading *rependit* for *deprehendit*.
2 The author is certainly omitting more than he includes. See *Process passim* (*Early Documents*, pp. 132–85).
3 The majority of those Clare cured during her life and after her death were children. This may be an outcome of her great concentration on the person of Jesus as the 'most holy and beloved child'.
4 Ortolana probably followed her daughters into the Order after the death of her husband. Miracles were attributed to her in life and after death, and according to one source she was later beatified. In the Franciscan martyrology her feast occurs on 2 January. For the play on her name, here amplified, compare chapter 1, note 3. Clare was the 'little plant' of Francis, his first offshoot. At Song of Solomon 4.12 the 'enclosed garden' is a metaphor for the new Israel.
5 This is Sister Benvenuta of Lady Diambra (*Process* II 16, III 10).
6 Sister Amata of Corozano, traditionally a niece of Clare's.
7 We know from the *Process* that this is Sister Benvenuta of Perugia, a friend

of Clare's during her stay in that city.

8 Lady Cristiana of Parisse, fifth witness in the *Process*. Her cure is attested by two other sisters.

9 The Latin says simply *locum*, 'the place'. The infirmary at St Damian's was above the refectory.

10 One of these was Sister Pacifica (*Process* I 10).

11 This is an allusion to the tree of life (the leaves of which 'were for the healing of the nations', Revelation 22.2), an image beloved of the Franciscan mystics.

Her Daily Instruction of the Sisters

36 Because she was clearly a teacher of the uneducated and the governess of young ladies, as it were, in the palace of the Great King, Clare moulded[1] them with such discipline and fostered in them such a love of holiness as can hardly be expressed in words. First she taught them to banish all noise from the realms of their minds, so that they might be able to cling to the mysteries of God alone. She taught them not to be affected by love for earthly relatives, and to forget their families and homes in order to please Christ. She encouraged them to disregard the demands of the mortal body and to curb the follies of the flesh with the reins of reason. She showed them how the treacherous enemy lays hidden traps for pure souls and tempts saints in one way, and the worldly in another. Finally, she wanted them to engage in some manual labour at certain hours[2] so that they should constantly be kindled afresh to perform their Founder's will through the exercise of prayer,[3] and so that, shunning apathy and negligence, they should banish all spiritual coldness with the fire of holy love. Nowhere was a greater observance of silence to be found, nowhere was the shining quality of every virtue more in evidence.[4] There was no frivolous talk, indicative of a frivolous spirit, nor any shallow discourse, which betrays a shallow mind. For the teacher herself spoke very little, and eloquently expressed the wishes of her heart in a very few words.

1 The Latin noun translated in the chapter title as 'instruction' is *informatione*, and the verb translated here as 'moulded' is *informabat*. *Informare* means basically to 'give shape to'. In Franciscan circles the term was, and is still, 'formation', which does not mean 'discipline' in our modern sense so much as 'training' and even 'learning'.

2 The *Rule* (chapter VII) stipulates 'after the Hour of Terce', which means 9.00 a.m. Clare writes: 'They must work in such a way that they banish idleness . . . yet do not stifle that spirit of holy prayer and devotion to which all temporal things must be subservient.'

3 St Benedict had warned his Order against the temptations of idleness, and St Francis (*Later Rule*, chapter 5) called it 'the enemy of the soul'.

4 *nusquam amplior et color et tenor omnis honesti* is variously translated by authors, some appearing to read *cultus* for *color*, some *timor* for *tenor*.

Her Keen Desire to Hear the Preaching of the Word

37 Through zealous preachers Clare provided her daughters with the nourishment of the word of God, and she herself derived from it as much benefit as they. For when she heard holy preaching she was filled with such joy, and so happy to hear the remembrance of her Jesus that once, when Brother Philip of Atri[1] was preaching, a most beautiful young boy[2] stood at her side and for the greater part of the sermon delighted her with his expressions of joy. And the sister who was given grace to see this apparition experienced a bliss beyond description at the sight. And though she was not formally educated,[3] Clare enjoyed hearing a learned sermon because she believed that the kernel of its teaching lay within the shell of its text, and this she would attend to with great discernment and savour with great relish. But she knew how to draw from the sermon of any preacher what was of spiritual benefit, for she understood that it was sometimes as prudent to pick a flower from a prickly thorn as to eat the fruit of a choice tree.

Once when Pope Gregory had forbidden any friar to go to

the monasteries of the Ladies without his permission,[4] the good mother, lamenting the fact that her sisters would now receive the food of holy doctrine more rarely, commented with a sigh: 'Let him take away from us all the friars in future, now he has taken from us those who provide us with the food of life.' And she at once sent all the friars back to the Minister,[5] not wishing to keep the questors to provide bodily nourishment when they had none to provide spiritual sustenance. But when Pope Gregory heard what she had done he immediately relaxed his prohibition, and left the matter in the hands of the Minister General.[6]

NOTES

1 Brother Philip the Long, from Atri in Abruzzo, was a very gifted preacher and accompanied Francis on his secret visits to Clare. Philip was one of those who preached at St Damian's, and in Francis' absence in the Middle East, he was appointed Visitator of the Poor Ladies.

2 See above on chapter 33, note 3.

3 Clare was not educated in the liberal arts, in the Trivium or Quadrivium (grammar, rhetoric, logic, plus arithmetic, geometry, astronomy and music): as a woman she had not been to university. But as the daughter of a noble family she would have been well educated at home. She was certainly more literate than Francis. No doubt the sermons she heard were given by the friars in the vernacular; but Clare could read and write Latin, and probably French too, as well as the local dialect. Bartoli (p. 6) calls her 'a not particularly cultivated woman', but her letters to Agnes of Prague (unless we are to think of her using secretaries who polished what she had dictated) reveal a writer who could rise to considerable heights, and one who was no stranger to the niceties of rhetoric.

4 In his Later Rule Francis forbids his friars to enter the monasteries of nuns without the special permission of the Apostolic See. By his bull *Quo Elongati* of 28 September 1230 Gregory IX applied this to the houses of Poor Clares. But Clare had always seen the two Orders in a special relationship, as a fraternity, and she relied on the friars for material and spiritual assistance, which Francis had promised her in his and their name (*Rule*, chapter VI). This obligation soon became a source of division among the friars.

5 I.e. the Minister Provincial, who exercised authority over the houses of an Order within a prescribed area.

6 The Minister General is the head of the Order.

38 The venerable abbess loved not only the souls of her daughters, but also looked after their physical well-being with the most loving care.[1] For often in the chill of night she herself would cover them as they slept, and she urged any she found who were unable to observe the austerities of the community to be content with a less rigorous regime. If any were assailed by temptation or beset by sorrow, as can happen from time to time, she would call them on one side and console them with tears of sympathy. Sometimes she threw herself at the feet of sisters who were troubled to ease the burden of their grief with a mother's caresses. Her daughters were more than grateful for her kindnesses to them, and dedicated themselves to her with utter devotion. Indeed, they honoured Clare as a mother for the deep love she gave them, revered her as a teacher in her office of superior, followed her as their guide in the path of virtue, and admired her as the spouse of God graced with every kind of holiness.[2, 3]

NOTES

1 The abbess was responsible for the health of all the sisters, and if Clare had ignored the demands of her own body, she was always preoccupied with the well-being of her sisters.

2 A finely weighted ascending tetracolon to conclude the paragraph. The author's clausulae are often studied and elegant.

3 Here in the Bollandists' version follow chapters 39–45, which contain two episodes which have intruded from other sources. (a) 39–42: St Clare's meal with St Francis and his friars at the Portiuncula; (b) 43–5: how Clare miraculously imprinted the cross on some loaves of bread.

Her Infirmities and Long Illness

39 For forty years Clare had run the course of sublime poverty, and at last, as her illnesses multiplied, she began to near the prize of her heavenly calling.[1] In her earlier years she had subjected herself to such rigorous penances that now her bodily strength failed, and a cruel sickness beset her later years, so that she who in good health had been enriched by the merits of her good works might now in her sickness be enriched by the merits of her suffering. For indeed, 'virtue is made perfect in weakness'.[2] How Clare's prodigious virtue was made perfect in her sickness is admirably illustrated by the fact that in her 28 years of unremitting illness, not a murmur of complaint was heard from her. In conversation she was always on some hallowed theme, gratitude was in every word she spoke. Though she was oppressed by the burden of her infirmities and seemed to be hastening towards her end, it was nevertheless God's will to delay her death until such time as she could be given fitting honour by the Roman Church, whose child she was, and most special daughter.[3] For while the Pontiff and Cardinals were still in residence at Lyons,[4] Clare's illness became more acute, and a sword of grief was plunged into the hearts of her daughters.[5]

40 Then one of the handmaids of Christ, a virgin dedicated to God, of the monastery of San Paolo of the Order of St Benedict,[6] had a vision: it seemed to her that she was with her sisters at St Damian's attending the Lady Clare in her sickness, and Clare was lying on a sumptuous bed. And as they all wept and tearfully awaited the passing of blessed Clare, a beautiful woman appeared at the bed-head and spoke to them in their grief. 'Do not weep, my daughters,' she said, 'for she will yet live.[7] She cannot die until the Lord comes with his disciples.' And sure enough, a short while after, the papal court arrived in Perugia. The Bishop of Ostia,[8] hearing of the deterioration in Clare's condition, came in haste from Perugia to visit the spouse of Christ, to whom he had been a father by virtue of his office, a benefactor by virtue of his solicitude, and a loyal and devoted friend by virtue of his most chaste affection. He nourished her on her sick-bed with the sacrament of the Lord's body, and nourished the other sisters too

with salutary words of consolation. Clare earnestly and tearfully begged the great Pontiff in the name of Christ to remember her soul and the souls of the other Ladies in his prayers.[9] But above all, she begged him to win for her from the Lord Pope and Cardinals the confirmation of her Privilege of Poverty. This the Bishop as a faithful supporter of her Order promised to do, and was as good as his word.[10]

A year later the Lord Pope moved with his Cardinals from Perugia to Assisi,[11] and the vision described above concerning the saint's passing was brought to fulfilment. For the Supreme Pontiff himself, who is above all men as he is below God, represents the person of the Lord, and at his side in close attendance stand the Lord Cardinals, like disciples, in the temple of the Church Militant.

NOTES

1 This was 1252, when Clare became so ill she was bed-ridden, and often seemed to be dying. The language used recalls that of 1 Corinthians 9.24 and Philippians 3.14.
2 2 Corinthians 12.9.
3 'Special daughter' (*filia specialis*) must allude to Clare's future canonization.
4 Innocent IV stayed at Lyons from December 1244 to April 1251 and returned to Italy later that year via Genoa, Milan and Bologna, settling at Perugia on 5 November, where he received a triumphant welcome.
5 Recalling Luke 2.35 (Simeon's prediction to Mary).
6 San Paolo at Bastia.
7 The Latin can mean either 'live' or 'conquer'. Both make sense, but on balance the former seems better in the context.
8 The Bishop of Ostia was now Cardinal Raynaldus Segni, Protector of the First and Second Orders, and later Pope Alexander IV.
9 Reading *tanto* for *tantum*, and *animas* for *famulas*.
10 For the Privilege of Poverty see above on chapter 14, note 8. Clare did not die, and a whole year passed in which nothing happened. It was not until 16 September 1252 that Cardinal Raynaldus wrote and agreed to the sisters following Clare's Rule. For the Pope's approval Clare had to wait until he came to Assisi to visit her.
11 He was there in 1253 from 27 April until 1 May for the consecration of the new Basilica of St Francis, then again from June to 6 October.

How Pope Innocent Visited Clare, Absolved Her and Blessed Her in Her Sickness

41 Divine Providence now hastened to fulfil its designs concerning Clare, and Christ hastened to lift his poor pilgrim to the palace of the heavenly kingdom. Clare already longed and

Innocent IV brings the Holy Sacrament to Clare on her deathbed

desired with all her heart to be 'freed from this mortal body'[1] and to see Christ reigning in the heavenly mansions, whom she, his poor handmaid, had followed with all her heart as the poor Man on earth. Her sacred limbs were exhausted by her long illness, and now she was stricken by a new infirmity which signalled her approaching summons to the Lord and prepared the way for her eternal health. Pope Innocent IV, of holy memory,[2] together with the Cardinals made haste to visit the handmaid of Christ, and since he was satisfied that her holiness of life surpassed that of all other women of our time, did not hesitate to honour her death with the papal presence.[3] He entered the monastery, went to her bedside and put his hand to her lips for her to kiss. Clare did so most gratefully, and with utmost reverence begged to be allowed to kiss the Pope's foot. So the Holy Father mounted a wooden footstool and graciously offered her his foot, and Clare, reverently inclining her head, pressed kisses upon it both above and beneath.[4]

42 Then with an angelic expression on her face she asked the Supreme Pontiff for absolution from all her sins. He replied: 'Would that I needed pardon as little as you,' and granted her the gift of perfect absolution and bestowed upon her the favour of his most ample blessing.[5] And when they had all gone, because she had received the sacred host that day from the Provincial Minister,[6] Clare raised her eyes to heaven, lifted her hands to God and in tears said to her sisters: 'Praise the Lord, my daughters, for Christ has today deigned to grant me a blessing so great that heaven and earth together could not equal it. Today,' she said, 'I have received the Most High Himself,[7] and been honoured by the sight of his Vicar.'[8]

NOTES

1 Compare Romans 7.24.
2 He died in 1254.
3 In fact two visits are recorded, one shortly after his accession, one just before Clare's death. Here the author conflates them into a single visitation, and so produces a fine scenario for an exemplary death.

4 Like Mary Magdalene kissing the feet of the Crucified.

5 What the author inexplicably omits is that Clare seized this occasion to press the Pope for confirmation of her Rule. The confirmation was granted by the bull *Solet Annuere* (9 August 1253), and received by Clare the day before she died. Sister Filippa (*Process* III) relates that Clare took the papal bull as she lay on her deathbed and kissed the seal. This bull was discovered only in 1893.

6 The author is at pains to make it clear that Clare has received absolution, made her communion, and received the Pope's blessing. All the liturgy of the dying is now complete.

7 That is, in the sacrament.

8 Vicar originally meant 'substitute': the pope is Christ's vicar on earth.

———

How She Replied to Her Weeping Sister

———

43 Clare's daughters, so soon to be orphaned, stood around their mother's bed, and a sword of bitter sorrow pierced their hearts.[1] No thoughts of sleep distracted them, nor could hunger tear them from her side: forgetful of rest and food their only comfort night and day was to weep. Among them the devout virgin Agnes, in a flood of salty tears, begged her sister not to depart and leave her. Clare replied to her: 'It is God's pleasure that I depart, dearest sister. But stop your weeping; because you will come to the Lord soon after me[2] and before I leave you the Lord will give you a great consolation.'

44 In the end it became clear that her final struggle was to last many days, and during this period the faith and devotion of people near and far were greatly increased. Clare was also honoured daily as a true saint by the frequent visits of Cardinals and other prelates. And, what is truly remarkable to relate, although for 17 days she was unable to take any food at all, she was given such vigour and fortitude by the Lord that she strengthened everyone who came to her in the service of Christ. For example,

when that kindly friar Brother Raynaldo encouraged her to be patient in her long martyrdom to so many infirmities, she replied without hesitation: 'My dearest brother, ever since I came to know the grace of my Lord Jesus Christ through his servant Francis, no pain has been distressing, no penance difficult, and no infirmity hard to bear.'[3]

45 But the Lord took pity on her and, as he was already standing, as it were, at the door, Clare asked for the priests and her spiritual brothers[4] to attend her and to recite the Passion of the Lord and passages of holy Scripture. When Brother Juniper appeared among them, that noble jester[5] of the Lord, who often uttered fiery passages from Scripture, she was suddenly filled with a new joy, and asked him if he had anything new to tell her of the Lord. As soon as Juniper opened his mouth, he breathed forth words like showers of flaming sparks from the furnace of his fervent heart, and the holy virgin Clare derived great comfort from his words. At length she turned to her weeping daughters, commended to them the poverty of the Lord and gratefully recalled all God's blessings. She blessed all those who were devoted to her, both brothers and sisters, and called down her richest benediction upon all the Ladies of the poor monasteries, both those present and those to come.[6] As to the rest, who could recount it without tears? The two blessed companions of blessed Francis stood at Clare's side; one of them was Angelo[7] who, though grieving himself, comforted the rest in their grief; the other, Leo,[8] pressed kisses on the bed where the saint lay dying. Clare's forsaken daughters were heartbroken at the departure of their loving mother, and as she slipped from them they followed her with their tears, knowing that they would never see her again. They grieved most bitterly that all their solace was to pass away with her, that they were to be left in the vale of tears without their teacher to comfort them any longer. Dignity alone kept them from doing violence to their bodies, and that barely; and the fact that they were not permitted to express their grief outwardly made the pangs of their misery even more keen. The rule of the cloister enjoined silence, but the violence of their sorrow wrung from them groans and sobs. Their faces were swollen with weeping, and the agony of their grieving hearts supplied floods of tears that were ever fresh.

46 But the most holy virgin turned her thoughts inwardly and whispered to her soul: 'Go in peace, for you have a good guide for your journey. Go,' she said, 'for he who created you has sanctified you and protected you always and loved you as tenderly as a mother loves her son. Blessed be thou, Lord,' she said, 'who created me.' And when one of the sisters asked her to whom she was speaking, she replied: 'I am speaking to my blessed soul.' And her glorious guide was not far off, for she turned to another of the sisters and said: 'My daughter, can you not see the King of Glory as I do?' But the hand of the Lord came down upon another[9] of the sisters, who, with her own bodily eyes, saw through her tears a glorious vision. Pierced as she was with a dart of keenest sorrow, she turned her gaze towards the doorway, and there, entering the house, came a throng of virgins in white garments, all of them wearing golden garlands on their heads.[10] Moving in their midst was one more resplendent than the rest, and from her crown, whose upper tier was pierced like a thurible, there radiated such a dazzling light that it turned night into day within the house. She advanced to the bed where the spouse of her Son lay, and bending most lovingly over her gave her a most sweet embrace. A mantle of miraculous beauty was brought forward by the virgins, and they all worked together eagerly as they covered Clare's body and decorated the bridal couch.[11]

So, on the day after the feast of Saint Lawrence,[12] Clare's most holy soul passed away to be crowned with its everlasting reward; the temple of her flesh was dissolved, and her spirit rose happily to heaven. And her passing from the vale of misery was blessed indeed, for it became for her the entrance to a life of blessedness. Now, for her earthly journey's meagre fare, she is happily seated at the table of the citizens of heaven; now for her sackcloth and ashes, she is blessed in the heavenly kingdom and clothed in a robe of imperishable glory.

NOTES

1 Compare Luke 2.35.

2 Agnes had been called to Assisi from Florence to attend her dying sister. According to Wadding she herself was to die some three months after Clare, aged 56.

3 Even at death's door Clare displays her characteristic tenacity and strength of will. She remained utterly convinced of her mission until the end.

4 Juniper, Angelo and Leo, Francis' earliest companions.

5 The reading of the manuscripts is *jaculator*, which means 'spearsman'. Possibly we should read *joculator*, meaning 'jester', 'jongleur' or 'minstrel'. In (admittedly later) Franciscan literature, Juniper is regularly depicted as a rather simple-minded bungler, 'God's fool'. His life is appended to the *Little Flowers*.

6 Various benedictions have survived in a variety of languages. None is regarded as indisputably authentic.

7 This is Brother Angelo Tancredi, who was of noble birth, traditionally one of the collaborators in the *Legend of the Three Companions*, an account of the life and miracles of St Francis.

8 Leo was one of Francis' closest companions, his secretary, nurse and confessor, and a lifelong friend of Clare. He died in 1270/1 and was buried beside his master.

9 Compare 2 Kings 3.15; Ezekiel 1.3.

10 Compare Revelation 7.9.

11 One manuscript adds: 'So she disappeared and withdrew heavenwards and none of those who saw her doubted that she was the very Mother of the Lord.'

12 That is on 11 August 1253. (The feast of St Lawrence is on 10 August.) Clare was about 60 years old. According to Sister Filippa (*Process* III 23) Clare spent the whole night of the day on which she died preaching to the sisters. Then she made 'such a beautiful and good confession' that Sister Filippa declared she had never heard anything like it. According to Sister Agnes, daughter of the mayor of Assisi (*Process* X 10), Clare's last prayer was the Prayer of the Five Wounds of Christ, and her last words, addressed to Agnes herself, were: 'Precious in the sight of the Lord is the death of his holy ones' (Psalm 116.15).

How the Roman Curia Flocked
with a Large Crowd of People to the
Funeral of the Virgin

47 News of the sudden passing of the virgin shook the entire population of the city. Everyone flocked to the place, men and women alike, in fact people flooded there in such great numbers that the city seemed deserted. Everyone proclaimed Clare a saint, one of God's elect, and as they uttered these words of praise many burst into tears. The Podesta[1] with a troop of knights and a great company of armed men kept close watch that evening and the whole of the night[2] so that the precious treasure that lay within should not be lost.[3] Next day the whole Curia was stirred into action: the Vicar of Christ together with the Cardinals arrived[4] and the whole city directed its steps towards St Damian's. And when the time came to celebrate the divine service and the friars had begun to say the Office of the Dead, the Lord Pope suddenly announced that it was the Office of Virgins that should be recited, not the Office of the Dead. It seemed as if he wanted to canonize Clare before her body had been given proper burial. But when the Bishop of Ostia,[5] that most eminent man, replied that such matters demanded more mature reflection, the Mass of the Dead was celebrated. Then, when the Supreme Pontiff and Cardinals and all the other gathered prelates were seated,[6] the Bishop of Ostia, taking as his theme the text 'Vanity of vanities',[7] eulogized this remarkable woman who had so despised vanity, in a memorable sermon.

48 Then the Cardinal Priests in deep devotion gathered round the precious bier and completed the customary rites over the virgin's body.[8] Finally, because they considered it neither safe nor seemly that so valuable a possession should be left at such a distance from the citizens,[9] the corpse was lifted up to the singing of hymns and songs of praise, and amid the braying of trumpets and solemn rejoicing it was carried with all honour to the church

of San Giorgio. For this is where the body of the holy father St Francis had first been buried[10] and it seemed predestined that he who had given a way of life to the virgin while she lived should also provide her with a resting-place in death. Subsequently a great concourse of people visited the tomb of the virgin, praising God and saying: 'Truly she was a saint! Truly, she who received such honours from her fellow men on earth now reigns in glory with the angels! O Clare, foremost of the Poor Ladies, you who led countless souls to repentance, countless souls to life, intercede for us with Christ!' After a few days,[11] Agnes herself was called to her espousal with the Lamb and followed her sister Clare into everlasting joy, where the two daughters of Sion, sisters in blood, in grace and in majesty give glory to God without ceasing. So in fact Agnes received the consolation which Clare promised her before she died. For just as, when her sister had gone before her, Agnes soon passed from the world to the cross; so too, while Clare was resplendent for her signs and wonders, Agnes soon followed her from the passing light of this world and awoke to God.

Through our Lord Jesus Christ, who with the Father and Holy Spirit[12] lives and reigns for ever and ever. Amen.

NOTES

1 The mayor of Assisi, who according to the *Verse Legend* brought seven knights.

2 Some time seems to have elapsed in which the mayor mustered his troops, perhaps because the city was celebrating a festa. August 11 is the feast of San Rufino, patron saint of Assisi.

3 The theft of relics was widespread, and the Perugians in particular were adepts at this. They had tried to kidnap Francis on his deathbed so that he could die in their city. His body had to be carefully guarded, and his final burial place was kept so close a secret that it was only rediscovered early in the nineteenth century. Pennacchi records a case as recent as 1809, when the people of Stroncone stole the corpse of their fellow citizen, Blessed Antony, from St Damian's, where he had died in 1461.

4 This was the greatest honour. When Clare died the pope happened to be in Assisi, and he chose to attend the funeral.

5 Cardinal Raynaldus, who was later as pope to canonize Clare.

6 Reading *considente* for *confidente*.

7 Ecclesiastes 1.2.

8 The *Verse Legend* (1405ff.) tells us that the prelates placed their pontifical rings in Clare's hand hoping to invest them with power.

9 The people of Assisi had been quick to take Francis' body from the Portiuncula; so now they took Clare's body away to safety within easy reach of the city (see Map 3).

10 It was at St George's, just outside the east wall of the city, that Clare had first heard Francis preaching, and here in a chapel attached to the church his body had rested from October 1226 to May 1228, when it was translated to the new basilica. This chapel is also where Clare's body lay until her new basilica, which enclosed the old church of St George's, was finished. In 1260 her remains were re-interred under the high altar there.

11 According to Wadding 97 days later. See on chapter 43, note 2.

12 Reading *Spiritu* for *Filio*.

———

PART TWO

THE MIRACLES CLARE WORKED AFTER
SHE PASSED FROM THE WORLD

$\longrightarrow$

49 The great wonders and miracles worked by the saints deserve great veneration, and depend upon the holiness of their character and the perfection of their lives.[1] John the Baptist indeed did no miracles at all,[2] but those who did miracles were no holier than John. For this reason the fame of the virgin Clare's most perfect life would suffice as evidence of her holiness, if it were not that the people, partly through lukewarmness, partly because of their devotion, sometimes demand something more. So just as while she lived Clare was clearly a saint through her merits, now that she has been received into the innermost realms of eternal splendour she continues to win marvellous renown in every corner of the earth through the glory of her miracles.[3] Since I am sworn to truthfulness and accuracy, my account of these miracles must be lengthy. But because of their vast number I am compelled to omit a great many.[4]

NOTES

1 The author's preamble is characteristic of a thirteenth-century trend in attitudes towards miracles: they are the fruits, not the sources, of sanctity (Bartoli p. 193). Moral strength is more important than 'juggling tricks'. However, people cry out for miracles ...
2 John 10.41.
3 Another play on Clare's name: *Clara – claritatis – luce – declaratur*.
4 Two witnesses in the *Process* state that there were 'many more' miracles, and one should not forget that most of the evidence at the author's disposal came from the *Process* where only five healings outside the monastery are attested.

$\longrightarrow$

50 There was a sick boy from Perugia named Giacomino who had nothing wrong with him physically but seemed to be possessed by a terrible demon. One moment he would hurl himself madly into the fire, the next he would dash himself onto the ground, or chew stones until he broke his teeth, or tear the flesh of his face in shreds and cover his body with blood. His mouth was twisted, he stuck out his tongue, and his limbs were often so entangled that his legs became entwined around his neck. Twice every day this madness took hold of the boy, and not even two men together could prevent him from taking off all his clothes. The aid of skilled physicians was sought, but none could be found who knew what advice to give. The boy's father Guidalotto, unable to discover any earthly remedy for his son's terrible affliction, had recourse to the merits of St Clare. 'O most holy virgin,' he prayed, 'O Clare, venerated by the whole world, I vow[1] my poor child to you and most humbly beseech you to cure him.' Full of faith he hurried to Clare's resting place with the boy and placing him on the virgin's tomb asked for her aid, and even as he prayed, was granted it. For the boy was instantaneously freed from his affliction, and never suffered another of his attacks.

51 Alessandrina of Fratta,[2] in the diocese of Perugia, was plagued by a most fiendish demon, and this demon had such power over her that he made her fly like a bird over a towering rock that jutted over the edge of the River Tiber. He also made her alight on a slender little branch overhanging the river and kept her dangling there like a child at play. What is more, for her sins she had completely lost the use of her left side, and had a withered hand, and though she frequently tried various medicines she could find nothing to help her. Finally she went to the tomb of the glorious virgin Clare with a contrite heart, and invoking her merits, she received a complete cure for all three of her afflictions.

Her withered hand was cured, her side was healed, and she was freed from the demon who possessed her.

At the same time another woman of the same place was cured before the sepulchre of the saint, being freed from a demon and a number of painful afflictions.

NOTES

1 In medieval times parents often promised to consecrate a cured child to God or secondarily to the saint they had invoked. The child had not necessarily to become a Franciscan or a priest, but was presumably supposed to live a godly life in gratitude. For this and similar vows, see Thomas of Celano's *First Life of St Francis*, SPCK 2000, pp. 142–3, n. 1.
2 Now Umbertide, a village some 16 miles north of Perugia.

A Man Cured of Fits

52 A young Frenchman who was attached to the Curia[1] suffered bouts of frenzy during which he lost all power of speech and his body became terribly agitated. It was almost impossible to restrain him, and he would injure himself horribly as he struggled with those who were trying to hold him down. Finally he was tied with ropes to a funeral bier and taken forcibly by some of his fellow countrymen to the church of St Clare, and put down before her tomb. And at once, through the faith of those who had brought him there, he was completely cured.[2]

The Healing of an Epileptic

Valentino of Spello[3] was so badly afflicted with epilepsy that he collapsed to the ground six times a day, no matter where he happened to be. He also had a palsied leg and was unable to walk with any freedom. He was put on an ass and taken to the tomb of

St Clare where he lay for two days and three nights. On the third day, without being touched by anyone, his leg gave out a loud crack and instantly he was cured of both of his infirmities.

A Blind Man Receives his Sight

Giacobello, said to be the son of a woman of Spoleto, had been blind for 12 years. He had to have someone lead him about, and was unable to walk anywhere on his own without falling down. Once, in fact, when he was left on his own for a while by his guide he had a nasty fall, broke his arm and wounded his head. One night he was sleeping near the bridge at Narni[4] when a woman appeared to him in a dream and said: 'Giacobello, why do you not come to me in Assisi and be cured?' When he got up in the morning, with trembling he recounted his vision to two other blind men, and they replied: 'We have heard of a lady[5] who died lately in the city of Assisi; and they say the hand of the Lord honours her tomb with the gifts of healing and many miracles.'

When Giacobello heard this, he acted swiftly; he set out for Assisi without delay and spent the night at Spoleto, where he again had the same vision. So he braced himself for the journey and pressed on even more quickly, so eager was he to regain his sight.

53 But when he arrived in Assisi he found such large crowds of people massing before the resting-place of the virgin that he had no chance of getting to the tomb. He was bitterly disappointed that he could not get inside the place, but with great devotion he laid his head upon a stone and went to sleep outside the entrance-way. And sure enough the voice came to him a third time. 'The Lord will bless you, Giacobello,' it said, 'if you can only get inside.' So, when he woke he began to beg the crowds to let him through for the love of God: he was in floods of tears, he

68

cried aloud, and kept repeating his pleas. Finally the people made way. Giacobello threw off his shoes, took off his garments, tied the straps of his boots round his neck,[6] and then, humbly approaching the tomb, fell into a light sleep. 'Get up,' blessed Clare told him. 'Get up, because you are cured.' At once he got up; his blindness had gone completely, and all his dimness of vision had disappeared. Through Clare he could see the light of day with utter clarity,[7] and he praised and glorified God and called on everyone to bless him for this amazing miracle.

NOTES

1 He would have been in the service of someone in the papal court, which had returned from France with a retinue of courtiers and pages, and was in Assisi from 12 August to 4 October 1258.
2 The author is giving a theological explanation of what happened: miracles occurring after a saint's death rely on the faith of those asking for them.
3 Spello is about six miles south-south-east of Assisi.
4 Narni is a hill on the Via Flaminia 20 miles north-west of Rieti (see Map 2). This would be the bridge over the River Nera.
5 Note that they did not even know Clare's name: the fame of her miracles had outstripped the fame of her holiness. Perhaps therefore this took place shortly after her death and before the new church was built in her honour.
6 An extremely penitential act: the blind man strips off everything. The word translated here by 'straps of his boots' could equally well mean 'belt' or 'cord'. A Franciscan friend tells me that he can remember older friars sometimes going to confession with their knotted cords strung round their necks as a sign of penance.
7 Another cluster of puns on the saint's name: *clare – Claram – claritatem – clarificat*. In France Clare is still invoked by people with eye problems.

The Curing of a Crushed Hand

54 A man from Perugia named Buongiovanni Martini had gone off with his fellow citizens to fight the men of Foligno,[1] and no sooner had battle been joined than he was struck by a boulder which hit him hard on the right hand and severely crushed it. In his anxiety to find a cure he spent a great deal of money on doctors, but nothing the doctors did could help him, so he was left with a hand that was useless and no good for any work at all. He hated having to carry this hand about as if it were not his own and being unable to use it, so he often considered having it amputated. But hearing of the miracles the Lord was deigning to perform through his servant Clare, he made a vow,[2] hurried off to the sepulchre of the virgin, offered her a waxen image of his hand[3] and lay down upon the tomb. And at once, even before he left the church, his hand was completely restored to health.

NOTES

1 Foligno is some ten miles south-east of Assisi on the road to Spoleto. We can date this conflict to May or June 1254. After the death of Frederick II the Perugians, who supported the pope, took it upon themselves to drive those who supported the emperor out of the neighbouring cities of Umbria.

2 Literally 'vowed a vow' (compare Genesis 28.20). The precise nature of his vow is not clear, but in Caxton's version, 'he avowed that he should visit her'.

3 It was a common practice in medieval times to offer wax representations of the body, or a part of it, at the tomb of a saint, in the hope of a cure.

The Healing of the Lame

55 A youth named Petriolo from the town of Bettona[1] had been wasting away for three years, indeed, his long illness had so drained him that he seemed no more than skin and bones. His chronic illness had also given him such a crippled back that he was perpetually bowed and doubled over, and could scarcely manage to get about even with a stick. His father consulted many doctors, especially those who were experts in mending broken bones. He was prepared to spend everything he had to get the boy well again. And when he was told by them all that there was nothing they could do to cure the boy's illness, he had recourse to invoking the aid of the new saint, of whose miracles he was hearing. The boy was carried to the place where the precious remains of the virgin lay, and he had not lain before her tomb for long before his prayers were granted and he was restored to perfect health. He stood up at once, straight-backed and sound of limb, walking and leaping and praising God,[2] and called on the crowds of people there to sing the praises of St Clare.

56 There was a ten-year-old boy from the village of San Quirico[3] in the diocese of Assisi who had been lame from his mother's womb.[4] He had emaciated legs, his feet turned inwards and he zigzagged as he walked, and if he fell down he could hardly get to his feet again. His mother had more than once vowed him to St Francis, but his condition had not improved. However, hearing of the glorious fame of the blessed Clare and her recent miracles, she carried the boy to her tomb. After a few days, his shinbones gave an audible crack and his limbs were restored to their proper alignment, and what St Francis did not give the boy for all the prayers of his mother, his disciple Clare granted him through her God-given power.[5]

57 A citizen of Gubbio[6] named Giacomo di Franco had a son five years of age whose feet were so weak he had never walked and he was quite unable to move about. He was ashamed of his son and regarded him as a public disgrace to his family, and a reproach to him personally.[7] The boy would sleep on the ground, crawl about in the ashes of the fire, and every now and then try to get up onto a bench,[8] but he always failed; for nature had given him the desire to walk but had simply denied him the ability. His parents commended the boy to the merits of St Clare and, to use their own words, promised that 'if he were restored to health by her, he would be St Clare's servant'.[9] Scarcely had this vow been uttered when the virgin of Christ cured her servant, and restored

to the boy who had been offered to her the ability to walk with ease. His parents at once hurried with him to the virgin's tomb and, as he leapt joyfully about, dedicated him to the Lord.

58 A woman called Plenaria from the town of Bevagna[10] had for a long time suffered from paralysis of the spine[11] and was unable to walk without the aid of a stick. But even with a stick she could not straighten her body, and she tottered about, dragging herself along as best she could. One Friday she had herself carried to the tomb of St Clare where, after pouring out a stream of fervent prayers to her, she soon gained the favour she had asked for in faith. She had been carried there by others, but the next day, Saturday, she went back home on her own two feet, completely cured.

NOTES

1 Bettona is about eight miles south-west of Assisi.
2 Compare Acts 3.8.
3 A small village near Bettona, now ruined.
4 Compare Acts 3.2.
5 Perhaps Clare's powers worked when those of St Francis would not because they were more recent. In the popular imagination, miraculous power was stronger if newer. Francis had now been dead for some years.
6 Gubbio is about 20 miles north of Assisi at the foot of Mt Ingino.
7 An interesting indication of medieval attitudes to sick people.
8 Reading *bancum* for *baculum*.
9 Literally 'a man of St Clare'. The child became, in effect, Clare's servant, and Clare became his *domina*, in a feudal relationship. (It was God, of course, who cured the child, and it was to God that they consecrated the child after the cure.) It is unclear exactly what obligations this involved: at the least the saint's 'man' would be expected to lead a devout life in future; perhaps on occasions this meant becoming a cleric, or entering the saint's Order.
10 Bevagna is a town in the Spoleto valley, about ten miles south of Assisi, and four miles south-west of Foligno. It was very near here that St Francis preached to the birds.
11 The woman's precise ailment is hard to identify. The Latin *contractionem renum* suggests paralysis of the loins, or lower back.

The Healing of Tumours of the Throat

A girl from Perugia had suffered great pain for a long time from tumours of the throat, which are commonly known as 'scrofula'.[1] No fewer than 20 swellings could be counted there, so many in fact that the girl's throat seemed larger than her head. Her mother often took the girl to the tomb of St Clare where she most devoutly implored the aid of the saint. Then one day, when the girl had lain all night before the sepulchre, she broke into a sweat, her swellings began to soften and then gradually to move. Indeed, in time, through the merits of St Clare, they cleared up so completely that not the slightest trace of them remained.

59 While St Clare was still in the flesh, Andrea, one of the sisters, had a similar illness in her throat. Now it is indeed strange that in the midst of so many glowing coals a soul as cold as Andrea's could lie hidden, and that in a company of wise virgins she should play the foolish one.[2] One night, wishing to force the swelling out through her mouth and by her own efforts to surpass the will of heaven, she squeezed her throat so hard she all but suffocated. But Clare knew of this at once by intuition. 'Run,' she told a sister; 'run as quickly as you can downstairs,[3] warm an egg and give it to Sister Andrea da Ferrara[4] to drink, then come back with her to me.' The sister ran off and found Andrea speechless and close to suffocation through the violence she had done herself. She did what she could to relieve her, then took her to her mother. 'You poor girl,' Clare said to her; 'you must confess those thoughts of yours to the Lord, because I know perfectly well what they are. I tell you, the Lord Jesus Christ will grant you the cure you wanted. But change your life for the better, for you are to suffer another infirmity from which you will not recover.' At these words Andrea felt the spirit of compunction, and she changed her way of life so that it was markedly improved. Then a short while after she had been cured of scrofula she passed away from another illness.

1 Scrofula is tuberculosis, especially of the lymphatic glands, and was known familiarly as 'the king's evil'.
2 Compare Matthew 25.4.
3 The sisters lived mostly upstairs, where the dormitory was (and originally also the front door, which was reached by a flight of steps suspended by chains). Presumably the animals were kept below.
4 Andrea is included among the 38 sisters listed for the year 1238 in the document known as The Mandate (*Early Documents* pp. 111–12).

People Rescued from Wolves

60 The countryside was frequently troubled by the savage ferocity of bloodthirsty wolves, which would often attack human beings and devour their flesh. Now there was a woman called Bona of Monte Galliano,[1] in the diocese of Assisi, who had two sons and one of them had been carried off by wolves. Scarcely had she finished mourning him when they came after her second son in another savage attack. While the mother was indoors doing some housework and the boy was walking outside, a wolf sank its teeth in him, gripped him by the neck and ran off as fast as it could to the woods with its prey. Some men who were in the vineyards heard the boy's screams and called out to the mother: 'See if your boy is in there with you! We have just heard some strange cries!' The mother, realizing her child had been carried off by wolves, raised her voice to heaven, and filling the air with her cries, called upon the virgin Clare for help. 'Holy and glorious Clare,' she said, 'give me back my poor boy! Give an unhappy mother back her darling son, because if you do not, I will drown myself!'[2] Her neighbours gave chase and found the child abandoned by the wolf in the wood, and a dog next to him licking his wounds. In its fury the wolf had first sunk its teeth into the boy's neck, then, the better to carry off its prey, it had fastened

74

its jaws around the boy's back, and in both places it had left the marks of a violent mauling. The woman's prayer was answered, and she hurried with her neighbours to the tomb of her protectress, showed the various wounds on her boy's body to all who wished to see them, and gave abundant thanks to God and St Clare.

61 A girl from the village of Cannara[3] was sitting in a field one fine day combing the hair of a woman whose head was in her lap. Suddenly a bloodthirsty wolf in search of prey ran swiftly and stealthily towards them. The girl saw it but, thinking it was a dog, was not afraid, and as she turned her attention to her friend's hair again, the cruel beast vented its fury on her, seizing her head in its great jaws and carrying its prey off into the woods. The woman was dumbfounded but got up at once and remembering St Clare cried: 'Help, St Clare, help! I entrust this girl to you in her hour of need!' And, wondrous to relate, the girl who was being carried off in the jaws of the wolf turned on the wolf and cried: 'You thief, do you dare take me any further, when I have been entrusted to such a virgin?' This reproach bewildered the wolf, which at once placed the girl gently on the ground and, like a thief caught in the act, scampered quickly away.

NOTES

1 This may be Monte Galgano, which is about seven miles north-east of Assisi. The area was densely forested and notorious for its packs of wolves, which preyed on cattle.

2 The woman cunningly uses blackmail. If Clare does nothing, she will lose two souls instead of one.

3 Cannara is in the lower Spoleto valley, seven miles south of Assisi on the Bevagna–Montefalco road. These are all very local miracles.

THE CANONIZATION OF THE
HOLY VIRGIN CLARE

—◆—

62 Now when talk of these miracles was circulating everywhere, and the renown of the virtues of Clare was becoming daily more widespread, and the world itself was waiting impatiently for the canonization of so great a virgin, the chair of St Peter was occupied by that most clement prince Alexander IV,[1] a man who was the friend of all holiness, the protector of all religious and the firm supporter of all religious Orders. Finally, moved by the great number of these miracles to treat Clare's case as exceptional, the Pontiff together with his Cardinals began to consider her canonization. The scrutiny of her posthumous[2] miracles was entrusted to eminent and prudent men[3] who were also instructed to discuss the marvellous things she had performed while living. As a result it was established that Clare, while she lived, had been the most shining example of every virtue; and after her death she was found worthy of veneration for miracles which were genuine and attested.[4]

A day was appointed for the ceremony,[5] and when the Cardinals had assembled, with a throng of Archbishops and Bishops as well as a crowd of clergy and religious, and in the presence of a number of learned and eminent men, the supreme Pontiff put this momentous business before them and asked for the judgement of the prelates. Their response was swift and unanimous. They said that Clare, whom God had glorified in heaven, should also be glorified on earth.

So, two years after her death, and close to the actual day of her passing, a huge gathering of prelates and all the clergy was convoked, and after preaching a sermon, the happy Alexander, to whom this grace had been reserved by the Lord, reverently and with utmost solemnity inscribed Clare in the catalogue of the saints, and solemnly declared that her feast day[6] should be celebrated by the whole Church. And he himself, together with the whole Curia, was first to celebrate it, and did so with the greatest pomp and ceremony.

Alexander IV and his cardinals affirm Clare's sanctity

All this took place in the main church at Anagni[7] in AD 1255, in the first year of the pontificate of Pope Alexander.

Praise be to our Lord Jesus Christ, who with the Father and Holy Spirit lives and reigns for ever and ever. Amen.

NOTES

1 Alexander IV was Cardinal Raynaldus dei Conti di Segni. He succeeded Innocent IV in 1254.

2 I have added the word 'posthumous' in the interests of clarity. The distinction between the *miracula in vita* and those *post mortem* is sharply drawn.

3 In the bull *Gloriosus Deus* (1 October 1253) the pope commanded Bartholomew, Bishop of Spoleto, to investigate the life and miracles of Clare. Bartholomew chose to assist him the Archdeacon Leonardo of Spoleto, Jacobo Archpriest of Trevi, Brothers Leo and Angelo (companions of Francis), Brother Mark (chaplain to St Damian's) and a notary. These went in November 1253 to St Damian's and interviewed under oath 15 of the sisters there, and the abbess. They also interviewed five lay people of Assisi who had known Clare and her family well. Their findings are transcribed in the *Acts of the Process of Canonization*, a document whose primacy as a source of information about the saint is unquestioned, and which was discovered only in 1920 in a fifteenth-century Italian version.

4 Note the cautious wording here, indicative of a change of attitude: miracles must be properly scrutinized; *per se* they were no longer proof of sanctity.

5 The precise day of Clare's canonization has been disputed, but the verdict of the most recent scholarship is 15 August 1255, two years and four days after her death. The eloquent bull of canonization ('*Clara claris praeclara*') was promulgated somewhere between 26 September and 19 October of that year.

6 Clare died on 11 August, the feast day of Assisi's patron saint, San Rufino; so her feast day was prescribed for the following day. (This feast was not promulgated within the Order of Friars Minor until five years later, in 1260.) As soon as her cult was given official recognition it met with resistance, especially within the Order of Friars Minor. In St Bonaventure's new official *Major Life* of St Francis, completed by 1262, Clare is mentioned only four times, and the Chapter of Paris in 1266 decreed that all other Legends be destroyed. No doubt this reticence was politically motivated. In his *Major Life* Bonaventure was trying to paint the sort of picture of Francis that the party then in power wished to disseminate, one that might smooth out differences between reformers and 'spirituals' within the Order. It was not the original Francis, of course, the real Francis whom Leo and Angelo had known: it was a watered-down version. And Clare had always insisted on living according to the earliest, most uncompromising Franciscan ideals.

7 Anagni is in Lazio, some 35 miles south-east of Rome.

PART II

The Form of Life of St Clare

INTRODUCTION

The Form of Life of St Clare (often referred to as her 'Rule') is the crowning achievement of her struggle to gain official recognition for the way of life which, under Francis' inspiration, she had chosen. She composed it between 1247 and 1252, and based it firmly on the Rule of Francis which had been approved in 1223; she also to some extent used those drawn up by Hugolino (1219) and Innocent IV (1247).

Hugolino's Rule of 1219, based on Benedictine practices, was an attempt to provide a more regular way of life for the growing numbers of women who, influenced by the preaching of the friars, were living the religious life in Tuscany, Umbria and Lombardy. This Rule was adopted by some houses, but never, so far as we know, by the Poor Ladies of St Damian's, whose unique status received official recognition in 1228 with the approval of the Privilege of Poverty (see *Legend* chapter 14, note 8; chapter 40, note 10).

In the 28 years between Hugolino's Rule and that of Innocent IV, a great number of monasteries were established on the lines of the Poor Ladies at St Damian's, and it seems that they were not content to profess the Benedictine Rule. So in 1247 Innocent IV composed his own Rule, adapting and adding to that of Hugolino, and basing it not on the Rule of Benedict, but on that of Francis. In it, however, among other things he insisted on the necessity of possessing communal property. Innocent's Rule was no more widely accepted than Hugolino's had been, and three years later he rescinded it.

It was clear to Clare that she must compose her own Rule. This she did, basing her prescription firmly on the Later 1223

Rule of Francis (see *Francis of Assisi: Early Documents*, edited by Regis J. Armstrong, J. A. Wayne Hellman and William J. Short, New City Press, 1999, pp. 99–106). Clare was the first woman in the history of the Church to compose a religious rule. Final confirmation of her Rule (the papal bull *Solet Annuere*), given on 9 August 1253, reached her the day before she died.

The original text was discovered in 1893 wrapped in an old habit of St Clare, and is now preserved in a reliquary in the Protomonastery at Assisi. At its head, in Innocent IV's own hand, are the words *Ad instar fiat S*: 'So be it.' ('S' is the signature of the pope, whose baptismal name was Sinibaldus. This is the formula of assent validating the document, which in normal circumstances would have been followed by the definitive document, with the name of the pope and his official seal at its head. Here the bull and the petition are the same document. Clare's request had no doubt been oral. Innocent IV visited Clare at the beginning of August in 1253, and composed the bull on his return, adding his signature at the head to ensure its validity.) Below is another inscription, also apparently in the pope's handwriting: *Ex causis manifestis michi et protectori mon[asterii] fiat ad instar* ('For reasons clear to me and to the protector of this monastery, so be it'). The 'clear reasons' must have been Clare's deteriorating condition, and this codicil was added to explain the unusual procedure: Clare was on her deathbed, and the pope was anxious to get the bull to her before she died. The document, dated 9 August 1253, was delivered by a friar from the convent where the pope had his residence and reached Clare the following day. As described elsewhere, when Clare took it in her hands she is said to have kissed it many times and died clutching it. She had fought all her life to preserve the true Franciscan ideals against men who had failed to understand them.

The *Rule* is one of the most important Franciscan documents extant, providing as it does a summary of the ideals of Francis written by his greatest disciple. The style is precise and official, and shows that Clare was well aware of the legal terminology of her times. Scholars assume that she must have had experts in canon law on hand when drafting it.

Every page speaks of personal experience; and throughout there is heard, insistently, the still small voice of common sense, of reason and of compassion (Clare had learnt that 'our bodies are not of brass'). A recurrent word in the *Rule* is 'discernment': the abbess in particular must use her discernment at all times, and the spirit of consultation and mutual responsibility is stressed as fundamental. The abbess and her vicaress are bound by exactly the same rules as the sisters, and their duty is to serve the community. The heart of the *Rule* is, of course, the section on poverty.

This is the way of life Clare fought for, and since her *Rule* was composed for St Damian's alone, the confirmation of the Holy See was a triumph for her because it was a final acknowledgement that St Damian's was unique.

(St Damian's, at least, was secure. But as soon after Clare's death as 1259, Alexander IV approved another Rule, that composed by blessed Isabelle of France for her monastery at Longchamp. However, the problem of the relations between the two Orders persisted: like Clare, Isabelle insisted on the closest relationship between the sisters and the Friars Minor, and increasingly it seemed that the majority of the friars were reluctant to accept this responsibility. In 1263, in an attempt peacefully to solve this problem and to clarify the confusion, Urban IV asked Cardinal John Gaetano Orsini (the future Nicholas III) to compose a new Rule for all Poor Clares except those of St Damian's and Prague (who were still to enjoy special privileges of poverty) and those adhering to the Isabelline Rule. In this new Rule, significantly, the friars were relieved of the sole responsibility for the spiritual support of the sisters, and the monasteries were given the right to acquire property in common. At a single stroke much that Clare had schemed and fought for was fatally undermined. Later, many monasteries of the Order of St Clare (as it came to be known) were to abandon this Rule of Urban IV and return to the Rule of their Foundress: some, the so-called 'Urbanists', still follow it today.)

For a full discussion of the Rule, including a comparison of Clare's Rule with those of Hugolino and Innocent, see Margaret Carney, OSF, *The First Franciscan Woman: Clare of Assisi and her Form of Life*, Franciscan Press, 1993.

The original text is continuous, without chapter divisions or headings, but the division into 12 chapters is ancient and convenient, and has been retained.

———

FORM OF LIFE OF THE POOR SISTERS

Innocent,[1] Bishop, Servant of the Servants of God, sends greetings and apostolic blessings to his beloved daughter in Christ, Clare, Abbess, and the other sisters in the monastery of St Damian's in Assisi.

It is the custom of the Apostolic See to grant the devout requests of its petitioners, and to give a favourable response to their just entreaties. Now we have received from you the humble plea that we confirm with our apostolic authority the form of life which was given you by blessed Francis and willingly accepted by you, according to which you are obliged to live together in unity of spirit and under a vow of the utmost poverty. Which form of life our venerable brother the Bishop of Ostia and Velletri saw fit to approve, as he himself explains at greater length in the letter he has written.[2] In answer therefore to your devout prayers, we ratify and approve what the said bishop has done in this matter, endorse it with our apostolic authority and formally confirm it with this present document, and attach hereto a transcript of the bishop's letter, reproduced word for word:

> Raynaldus, by God's mercy Bishop of Ostia and Velletri, sends greetings and a fatherly blessing to his dearest mother and daughter in Christ, the Lady Clare, Abbess of St Damian's in Assisi, and to her sisters, both present and future.
>
> Beloved daughters in Christ, inasmuch as you have spurned all worldly vanities and pleasures, and following in the steps of Christ himself and his most holy Mother have chosen to live enclosed[3] and to serve the Lord in utmost poverty so that you can engage in his service in freedom of soul, we approve this your holy form of life, and desire with fatherly affection freely to grant a favourable

response to your wishes and holy desires. Therefore, acceding to your pious prayers, we confirm in perpetuity this form of life and its way of living in holy unity and utmost poverty that your blessed father St Francis, both by word of mouth and in writing, gave you to observe, and on the authority of the Lord Pope as well as on our own authority we confirm it for all of you now living and for all who follow you, and we formally ratify it with this present document.

This form of life is as follows:

NOTES

1 Innocent IV, pope from 1243 to 1254.
2 Cardinal Raynaldus (whose letter is reproduced below), who became Pope Alexander IV in 1254. Ostia is at the mouth of the Tiber; Velletri is about 22 miles south-east of Rome.
3 The word *clausura* ('enclosure', 'claustration') does not occur in Clare's own writings. Clearly the issue of claustration was more important for the hierarchy of the Church outside than for Clare living on the inside, for whom poverty and mutual charity were the basis of community life. Claustration was indeed a source of tension between the Poor Ladies and Pope Gregory IX. (See Rule chapter II: Clare always allows a sister to leave the monastery *if there is good reason*.)

Chapter I

In the Name of the Lord.
Here Begins the Form of Life of the
Poor Sisters

The form of life of the Order of Poor Sisters, which was given them by blessed Francis,[1] is this: to observe the Holy Gospel of Our Lord Jesus Christ by living in obedience, without property, and in chastity.[2] Clare, unworthy servant of Christ and the 'little plant' of the most blessed Father Francis, promises obedience and reverence to the Lord Pope Innocent and his canonically elected successors and to the Roman Church. And just as at the beginning of her conversion she and her sisters promised obedience to blessed Francis, so she promises the same unfailing obedience to his successors. And the other sisters shall be bound always to obey the successors of blessed Francis[3] and of Sister Clare and the other abbesses canonically elected to succeed her.

NOTES

1 Clare states at the outset that it was St Francis who, by giving her a 'form of life', was the founder of the Order. Note also the title of 'Poor Sisters' (not 'Nuns', or 'Ladies') by which Clare associates her community with that of St Francis. (See on *Legend*, chapter 10, note 8.) 'Sisters of St Clare' became the normal style after her death.
2 In contrast to Innocent IV's Rule, Clare nowhere prescribes a detailed formula of profession.
3 Again Clare stresses the links between her community and the friars.

Chapter II

Those Who Wish to Accept This Life and How They Are To Be Received

If anyone is inspired by God to come to us wishing to accept this life, the abbess[1] is bound to seek the consent of all the sisters, and if the majority agrees, she may receive her after first obtaining the permission of our Protector, the Lord Cardinal.[2] And if she considers that this person should be received, she must carefully examine her or have her examined on the subject of the Catholic faith and the sacraments of the Church. And if the candidate believes all these things and is willing faithfully to confess them and to observe them steadfastly to the end; and if she has no husband (or, if she has a husband,[3] he has already entered the religious life with the authority of the bishop of the diocese, and has already made a vow of continence), and if there is no impediment to her observance of this life by reason of old age or mental or physical infirmity, then let the tenor of our life be clearly explained to her. And if she proves suitable, she should be read the words of the holy Gospel that tell her to go and sell all she possesses and be sure to give it to the poor. But if she cannot do this, her good will shall be sufficient. The abbess and her sisters should take care not to concern themselves with her worldly goods, so that she may be free to do with her possessions whatever the Lord inspires her to do. If, however, some guidance is needed in this, let them send her to some prudent and God-fearing men and let her goods be distributed to the poor on their advice.

After this, her hair shall be cut off round her head,[4] she shall put aside her secular clothes, and she shall be allowed three tunics and a mantle.[5] Thenceforth she shall not be permitted to leave the monastery except for some useful, reasonable, obvious and approved purpose.[6] At the end of her year of probation she shall be received into obedience and promise to observe our rule of life and our poverty. No-one shall be veiled during her period of probation. The sisters may also have scapulars[7] for the sake of ease and propriety when engaged in service and labour. But let the abbess use her discretion in providing them with clothing as seems necessary, taking into account the individual sisters, and the time of year and the climate of the region where the monastery is located.

Young girls who are received into the monastery before the proper age for profession should have their hair cut off round their heads, and when they have put aside their secular clothing they should be dressed in whatever religious habit the abbess deems appropriate. But when they reach the proper age, they should make their profession dressed in the same way as the others. And for these younger ones, as for the other novices, the abbess shall carefully select from among the most discerning sisters in the whole monastery a Novice Mistress who is to school them thoroughly in holy conduct and seemly behaviour according to the form of our profession. The same procedure should be followed in the examination and reception of the sisters who serve outside the monastery.[8] These sisters may wear shoes. No-one may take up residence with us in the monastery unless she has been received according to the form of our profession.[9]

And for love of the most holy and beloved Child[10] who was wrapped in mean little swaddling clothes and laid in a manger, and of his most holy Mother, I implore, I beg and beseech my sisters always to clothe themselves in garments that are poor.[11]

NOTES

1 See on *Legend*, chapter 12, note 2.

2 Clare insists on consultation at the outset: the sisters must be agreed, and obtain the permission of the Cardinal Protector.

3 Neither Hugolino's nor Innocent's Rule mentions the possibility of the entry into religion of a woman already married.

4 The tonsure is a rite of passage marking separation from the world, and a sign of penance marking a commitment to God. The act freed a person from the authority of the family and placed him or her under the protection of the Church.

5 The tunic was a loose-fitting outer garment; the mantle was a cloak provided for colder weather.

6 Even after profession Clare allows a sister to leave the enclosure if there is good reason. Hugolino's Rule permitted this only for the purpose of founding a new monastery.

7 Literally 'little mantles' (*mantellulas*). Presumably this refers to scapulars, which were sleeveless or short-sleeved garments used by the sisters when working.

8 Hugolino talks of 'servants' as opposed to 'sisters'. Generally in women's monasteries there were two categories of sisters: those better educated (and usually better born) who devoted themselves to prayer; and the 'lay sisters', who worked to provide the practical necessities of the monastery. But Clare envisaged no such division: she always worked herself, as did all the sisters at St Damian's.

9 In the Middle Ages women of noble families who could not marry often entered monasteries and lived there with their retinues in secular style. This would hardly have suited the life at St Damian's.

10 Clare is using the words Francis himself used in a hymn he wrote in the Office of the Passion (see *Omnibus* pp. 140–55).

11 'Poor' here means cheap and ordinary.

Chapter III

The Divine Office;
Fasting; Confession and Communion

The sisters who can read may possess breviaries for the recitation of the Divine Office, and this they shall do according to the custom of the Friars Minor, reading the Office, not chanting it.[1] If they are on occasion for some good reason unable to recite the canonical hours by reading them, they may, like the sisters who cannot read, say the paternoster. Those sisters who cannot read shall say 24 paternosters for Matins, 5 for Lauds, 7 for each of the Hours Prime, Terce, Sext and Nones; but 12 for Vespers, and 7 for Compline. For the dead they shall also say 7 paternosters with the *Requiem Aeternam* at Vespers, and 12 for Matins; while the sisters who can read are obliged to recite the Office of the Dead. When a sister of our monastery dies, they are to say 50 paternosters.

The sisters shall fast at all times[2] of the year. But at Christmas, on whatever day it falls, they may eat twice. The younger sisters, those who are weak and those who serve outside the monastery, the abbess may treat with compassion, and dispense from this obligation, as she sees fit.[3] But in time of obvious necessity, the sisters shall not be obliged to fast bodily.

The sisters shall make their confession, with the leave of the abbess, at least 12 times a year, and when doing so they must take care to speak only such words as are relevant to their confession and the salvation of their souls. They shall receive communion seven times a year, at Christmas, on Thursday in Holy Week, on Easter Day, at Pentecost, on the Assumption of the Blessed Virgin, on the feast of St Francis, and the feast of All Saints.[4] In order to give communion to the sisters both healthy and sick the chaplain is permitted to celebrate Mass within the monastery.

NOTES

1 Clare is providing an alternative way of prayer for the less educated sister, just as Francis had to provide for his illiterate brothers. The Friars

Minor wanted a simple way of reciting the Office so that they had more time for prayer and meditation. They recited the Divine Office according to the usage of the papal court (except for the Psalter, which was the Gallican Psalter in use everywhere outside Rome) and the Poor Ladies perhaps adopted the same practice.

2 That is, not merely during the two Lents (on fasting in general see above on *Legend*, chapter 18, note 4). Francis had permitted the fast to be broken (either by eating otherwise unauthorized fare or by eating more than one meal a day) on Sundays and at Christmas.

3 Again the abbess may use her discretion to exercise lenience.

4 Clare's prescription in this respect (as in the matter of e.g. abstinence) was not strict according to the standards of the time. The Beguines, for instance, sometimes made their communion daily.

Chapter IV

The Election and Office of the Abbess; the Chapter; the Officials and Discreets

In the election of the abbess the sisters shall be bound to observe the rules prescribed by canon law.[1] They shall as quickly as possible send for the Minister General of the Order of Friars Minor or the Minister Provincial, so that through the word of God he may engender in them a spirit of perfect peace and a desire for the common good in the coming election. No-one shall be elected abbess who is not a professed sister; and if a sister who is not professed should be elected or is appointed in some other way, the sisters are not to obey her unless she first professes our form of poverty.

At her death the sisters shall elect another abbess. If at any time it becomes clear to all the sisters that the elected abbess is incapable of serving and is not benefiting the whole community, the same sisters are bound as soon as possible to elect another as abbess and mother according to the above procedure.

The sister who is elected must bear in mind the responsibility she has taken upon herself, and to whom she will have to render an account of the flock committed to her.[2] She shall also strive to lead the others more by her virtues and holiness of life than by relying on the deference due to her office, so that the sisters may be inspired by her example to obey her through love rather than fear. She should avoid favouritism, for by loving one more than the others she may give offence to the whole community.

She shall console those sisters who are in distress and be the last refuge of those who are troubled, for if the weak find no healing remedies with her they may become prey to the sickness of despair.

She shall preserve the life of the community in all things, but especially in everything to do with the church, the dormitory, the refectory, the infirmary, and in the matter of dress. Her vicaress[3] shall do likewise.

At least once a week the abbess is obliged to call her sisters together in the Chapter, where she, as well as the sisters, shall humbly make public confession of their sins and omissions. And the abbess shall there discuss with all her sisters anything which concerns the welfare and reputation of the monastery; for the Lord often reveals what is best to the least of us.[4]

No heavy debt shall be incurred save with the consent of all the sisters and for some manifest necessity; and this should be done through a procurator.[5] But the abbess and her sisters shall beware of receiving anything for safekeeping in the monastery; for doing this often gives rise to disputes and scandals.[6]

In order to preserve the bond of mutual love and peace, all the officials of the monastery shall be elected by the common consent of all the sisters. In the same way, at least eight sisters shall be elected from the most discerning women in the whole monastery, whose advice the abbess shall always be bound to take in all matters concerning our way of life. But the sisters may, and must, if it seems to them desirable and expedient, remove the officials and discreets[7] from office and elect others in their place.

1 Clare is careful to stipulate an observance of canon law (something which none of the preceding Rules had specified).
2 The office was for life, unless the elected sister proved in some way incompetent.
3 The vicaress is the abbess' deputy.
4 Compare Matthew 11.25; St Benedict's Rule has 'younger': Clare writes 'least'.
5 The procurator was the person who managed the business of the monastery.
6 No doubt Clare had some experience of this during her long years at St Damian's.
7 The office of the discreets (the Latin means simply 'those [women] of discernment'), the abbess' team of counsellors, is apparently an innovation of Clare's. It is today a normal term in monastic houses. The council of eight is termed the *discretorium*.

Chapter V

Silence: the Parlour and the Grille

From the Hour of Compline until Terce the sisters shall keep silence,[1] with the exception of those serving outside the monastery. They shall also keep continual silence in church, in the dormitory, and while eating in the refectory.[2] But in the infirmary the sisters are always permitted to speak as seems necessary to them in comforting and caring for the sick. But wherever they are they should always convey what they need to say briefly and in a low voice. No sisters may speak in the parlour[3] or at the grille[4] without the permission of the abbess or her vicaress. When they are granted permission, they must not presume to speak in the parlour unless two other sisters are present and within hearing. Nor shall they presume to approach the grille unless accompanied by at least three sisters appointed by the abbess or her vicaress from among the eight discreets, who were elected by all the sisters to advise the abbess. The abbess and her vicaress shall themselves be bound to observe these same restrictions. Only on rare occasions should anyone speak at the grille, and absolutely never at the door. A curtain should be hung inside the grille, which may not be removed except when the word of God is being preached or a sister is speaking to someone on the other side.[5] The grille shall also have a wooden door tightly secured by bolts and bars, and with two separate iron locks, so that it can be locked, especially at night, with two keys, one of which shall be kept by the abbess, and the other by the sacristan. This door should always be kept locked except when the Divine Office is in progress, or for the reasons mentioned above. No sister must on any account speak to anyone at the grille either before sunrise or after sunset. There should always be a curtain in position inside the parlour, and it may not be removed.[6]

During the Lent of St Martin and the Greater Lent no-one shall speak in the parlour except to the priest during confession or for some other obvious necessity, which shall be left to the discretion of the abbess or her vicaress.

NOTES

1 That is, during the night (not, as Hugolino had prescribed, permanently).
2 Because the refectory could be used for other purposes.
3 Innocent (*Rule* chapter 9) had wanted the parlour to be either in the chapel itself, or (better) outside the chapel but within the enclosure.
4 The grille was a perforated metal screen through which speaking could take place. Clare envisages two grilles in the monastery: one in the parlour, and the other separating the sisters' choir from the church. The latter is referred to here.
5 The curtain can be drawn aside when necessary. Innocent IV did not wish the sisters to be seen at all.
6 Neither Hugolino nor Innocent had gone so far in their Rules. Perhaps in giving such detailed and precise prescriptions Clare wished to distance her community from the large numbers of minoresses and women preachers wandering through Italy unrecognized and without a formal rule.

Chapter VI

The Vow of Poverty

After the Most High Heavenly Father deigned to enlighten my heart by his grace to do penance following the example and teaching of our most blessed Father Francis, shortly after his own conversion, I together with my sisters voluntarily promised him obedience.[1] And when the blessed Father observed that we did not fear any poverty, toil, suffering, humiliation or worldly contempt, indeed that we considered them a cause for great rejoicing, in his compassion[2] he wrote a form of life for us, which is as follows:

> Because you have been inspired by God to make yourselves daughters and handmaids of the Supreme and Most High King, our Heavenly Father, and have espoused yourselves to the Holy Spirit by choosing to live according to the perfection of the Holy Gospel, I agree, and hereby solemnly promise, both in my own name and in that of my brothers, that I will always have the same loving care and special concern for you as I have for them.[3]

This promise he kept faithfully all his life and he wished it to be kept always by his brothers. And so that neither we nor those who came after us should deviate from the life of most holy poverty we had embraced, shortly before his death he wrote to us again with his last wishes:

> I, the insignificant brother Francis, wish to follow the life and poverty of Our Lord Most High Jesus Christ, and his Most Holy Mother, and to persevere in this to the end. And I urge you, my Ladies, I beseech you always to live this most holy life and to persevere in poverty. Be on your guard against listening to anyone whose teaching or counsel may cause you ever to depart from it in the slightest degree.

And just as I and my sisters have always been at pains to preserve the vow of holy poverty which we have made to the Lord God and to blessed Francis, so too the abbesses who succeed me in office and all the sisters must observe it scrupulously to the end: that is to say, they shall not receive or hold any possession or property (or even anything that might reasonably be termed property) either directly or through a third party, except as much land as the monastery needs for its decent seclusion.[4] And this land shall not be cultivated except as a garden for the use of the sisters.

NOTES

1 Suddenly the Rule becomes personal and autobiographical. Significantly we are at the heart of Clare's form of life: the section on poverty (chapters VI–VIII).
2 The same word could mean 'piety'.
3 Clare reproduces Francis' Form of Life and Last Will to underline his role as founder of her Order, and to stress the right of the Poor Ladies to the assistance of the friars now and for all time.
4 *honestate et seclusione*: I have taken these two words together, as hendiadys. *Honestas* is another word recurrent in Clare's writing. The underlining idea is one of 'appropriateness'. Here the phrase seems to indicate 'a fitting seclusion'. Clearly it was appropriate that a community of sisters should exist independently.

Chapter VII

Work and Alms

Those sisters who by the grace of God are able to work, shall after the Hour of Terce[1] work faithfully and devotedly at something which is appropriate to a life of virtue and which is useful to the community. They must work in such a way that they banish idleness, which is the enemy of the soul, yet they do not stifle that spirit of holy prayer and devotion to which all temporal things must be subservient.[2]

And all the handiwork that the sisters are to do must be assigned to them in the presence of the whole community in Chapter by the abbess or her vicaress.

Let the same be done if any alms have been sent by anyone for the needs of the sisters, so that the appropriate prayers for these benefactors be proposed before the whole community. And let all such gifts be distributed for the common good by the abbess or her vicaress, acting on the advice of the discreets.

1 That is, after 9.00 a.m.
2 See *Legend*, chapter 36 and note 3. The sisters were to engage in something as a normal daily occupation. Clare herself wove and spun, sewed and embroidered. This was not a commercial venture (as it was for the Humilati and the Beguines, for example, who were closely involved in the wool and cloth trade): the handiwork was not sold, but perhaps distributed as gifts in exchange for alms.

Chapter VIII

The Sisters Shall Not Acquire Anything for Themselves; the Begging of Alms; Sisters Who Are Ill

The sisters shall own no private property, whether a house or land or anything else. And as pilgrims and strangers in this world, serving the Lord in poverty and humility, they shall confidently send for alms. And they should not be ashamed to do so, because the Lord made himself poor in this world for our sake. This is the ideal of utmost poverty which has established you, my dearest sisters, as heiresses and queens of the kingdom of heaven. It has made you poor in the things of this world, but richly endowed you with spiritual gifts. Let that be your allotted path in life which leads to the land of the living.[1] Cleave to it with all your strength, my beloved sisters, and for the name of Our Lord Jesus Christ and his most Holy Mother, never desire to have anything else under heaven.

No sister shall be permitted to send letters or receive anything or give anything away outside the monastery without the permission of the abbess. Nor shall she be permitted to possess anything except what the abbess has given her or permitted her to have. If she is sent something by her family or friends, the abbess shall let it be given to her, and if it is something she needs, she may use it; if it is not, she shall give it charitably to a sister who does need it. But if any money[2] is sent her, the abbess, on the advice of her discreets, shall use it to buy something the sister needs.

As for the sisters who are sick, the abbess is obliged to do all she can, both by careful personal inquiry and by consulting the other sisters, to find out what counselling,[3] or what foods or other things are needed for the treatment of their infirmities, and to provide for them lovingly and compassionately so far as the resources of the monastery permit.[4] For all the sisters are bound to serve and look after the sick exactly as they would wish to be cared for if they themselves were suffering from some illness. Let each of them confidently make known her needs to another. If a mother loves and cherishes her earthly daughter, how much more deeply should a sister love and cherish her spiritual sister?

The sick may lie on mattresses filled with straw and have feather pillows for their heads, and those who need them may have woollen socks and coverlets. When sick sisters are visited by people from outside the monastery, they may each reply to their visitors with a few kindly words. But the other sisters who have permission to speak to people entering the monastery must not presume to do so except in the presence and within the hearing of two sisters of discernment[5] appointed by the abbess or her vicaress. The abbess and her vicaress are themselves bound by these same restrictions.

NOTES

1 Compare Psalm 142.5.
2 Clare uses the Latin word indicating a small amount of money.
3 A typically shrewd amplification of former regulations.
4 The abbess and her sisters would have to be accomplished nurses. Clare

was herself ill for many years and is at pains to provide for the sick in her community.

5 It is uncertain whether these chaperones had the formal office of discreet, or were merely women chosen for their discernment.

Chapter IX

The Penance to be Imposed on the Sisters When They Sin; Sisters Who Serve outside the Monastery

If at the instigation of the enemy any sister commits a mortal sin against the form of our profession, and after two or three warnings from the abbess or the other sisters does not mend her ways, for as many days as she remains obdurate she shall eat bread and water[1] on the floor of the refectory before all the sisters. And if the abbess sees fit, her punishment shall be even more severe. And so long as she refuses to yield, the sisters shall pray that the Lord may enlighten her heart to do penance. But the abbess and her sisters must take care not to become angry or anxious when anybody sins, because anger and anxiety make it difficult to be charitable, both for themselves and for others.

If it should ever happen (which God forbid) that, through some remark or gesture, trouble or enmity should arise between one sister and another, the sister who caused the trouble should at once, before she offers the sacrifice of prayer before the Lord, not only humbly prostrate herself at the other sister's feet and beg her pardon, but also ask her, in all sincerity, to intercede for her with the Lord that he may forgive her. The other sister must be mindful of the saying of Our Lord 'If you do not forgive from the heart, neither will your Heavenly Father forgive you',[2] and must freely forgive her sister all the wrong she has done her.

The sisters who serve outside the monastery may not remain long outside unless required to do so by some manifest necessity. And they must comport themselves with decency and speak little,

99

so that their behaviour provides a constant example to all who see them. And they must take the greatest care to avoid any meetings or conversations with others that may look suspicious. They may not be godmothers either of male or female children in case this leads to gossip or trouble. They must not presume to bring the gossip of the outside world into the monastery. And they are strenuously forbidden to repeat outside the monastery anything that is said or done inside that might cause scandal. If, however, any sister should offend on either of these counts through naivety, the abbess may use her discretion to impose a lenient penance on her. But if this sin is repeated through vicious habit, the abbess must, after consultation with her discreets, impose on her a penance appropriate to the seriousness of the offence.

NOTES

1 Clare's Rule is in fact extremely moderate in this respect compared with some contemporary monastic practices.
2 Compare Matthew 6.15; 18.35.

—◆—

Chapter X

The Admonition and Correction of the Sisters

—◆—

The abbess shall visit her sisters and admonish them and correct them humbly and charitably, never ordering them to do anything which is against their conscience or the form of our profession. But the sisters, who are under her, must remember that for love of God they have renounced their own wills. Therefore they are strictly bound to obey their abbesses in all those things which they have vowed to the Lord to observe and which are not against their conscience or the form of our profession.

The abbess, however, must enjoy such familiarity with them that they can speak to her and act towards her like mistresses to a servant. For ideally the abbess should be the servant of all the sisters.[1]

I urge and entreat the sisters in the Lord Jesus Christ to guard against all pride, vainglory, envy, avarice, and all care and anxiety about this world, and to beware of backbiting and resentment, conflict and discord.[2] Let them always be zealous to preserve among themselves that unity of mutual love which is the bond of perfection.[3]

Those sisters who are unable to read should not be anxious to learn. Let them concentrate instead on what they should desire above all else: to possess the spirit of the Lord at work within them, making them holy; to pray to him always with a pure heart; to be humble and patient in time of trouble or sickness; and to love those who persecute us, slander and accuse us. For the Lord says: 'Blessed are those who suffer persecution for righteousness' sake, for theirs is the kingdom of heaven.' 'But he that endureth to the end, he shall be saved.'[4]

NOTES

1 St Elizabeth of Hungary (1207–31) was another nobly born servant-saint like Clare who refused to let her servants call her 'mistress', wove wool for the poor, and made clothing for the friars.
2 Clare bases her text on Francis' Later Rule, but she goes further.
3 Compare Colossians 3.14.
4 Matthew 5.10; 10.22.

━━━━━►

Chapter XI

Guarding the Enclosure

━━━►

The portress must be of mature character, and discerning, and of a suitable age, and during the day she shall stay in an open cell without a door. She should also be assigned a suitable companion who can, when necessary, replace her and perform all her duties.[1]

The monastery door must be fastened securely with bars and bolts, and by two separate locks, so that, especially at night, it can be locked with two keys, of which the portress shall keep one, and the abbess the other. During the daytime the door must on no account be left without an attendant, and must be firmly locked with one key. The portress and her companion must be on their guard and take the utmost care to ensure that the door is never left open, but when this is unavoidable it must be opened no more widely than is strictly necessary. The door must on no account ever be opened to anyone wishing to enter unless they have been given leave by the Supreme Pontiff or our Lord Cardinal.

The sisters must not allow anyone to enter the monastery before sunrise or to remain inside after sunset, unless forced to do so by some manifest, reasonable and inevitable cause.[2] If any bishop is given permission to celebrate Mass within the monastery for the blessing of an abbess or for the consecration of one of the sisters as a nun or for some other reason, let him be content with as few companions and assistants as possible, and these should be men of proven virtue.

When it is necessary for men to enter the monastery to carry out some work, the abbess must be sure to station some suitable person at the door who will open the door only to the men authorized to do the work, and no-one else. On such occasions all the sisters must take the greatest care not to be seen by those who enter.

NOTES

1 Clare's prescriptions in this section are more precise and strict than those of previous Rules. Perhaps this was the fruit of her experience at St Damian's.
2 Once again the ultimate decision is left to the discretion of the sisters.

Chapter XII

The Visitator, the Chaplain and the Cardinal Protector

Our Visitator[1] must always belong to the Order of Friars Minor, and be chosen and appointed by our Cardinal.[2] And he should be a man well known for his integrity and virtue. His duty shall be to correct any excesses committed against the form of our profession, whether by the abbess, who is the head, or by the sisters, who are the members of the community. He should stand in a public place where he can be seen by others, and address his remarks either to several sisters at once, or to individuals, as seems best to him, about anything pertaining to his visitation.

We also ask as a favour of the same Order, for the love of God and blessed Francis, graciously to grant us a chaplain with one companion, a cleric of good reputation and proven discretion, and two lay brothers devoted to a life of holiness and virtue, to assist us in our poverty, such as we have always had through the compassion of the same Order of Friars Minor.[3]

The chaplain may not enter the monastery without a companion. When they enter, they must stay in an open place where they can always see each other and be seen by others. They may enter the monastery to hear the confession of the sick who cannot go to the parlour, to give them communion, to administer Extreme Unction, and to pray for the dying. For funerals and solemn Masses for the dead, moreover, for the digging or opening of a grave, or closing it afterwards, the appropriate number of suitable people may enter at the discretion of the abbess.

Finally, the sisters are strictly obliged always to accept as their Governor, Protector and Corrector, that Cardinal of the Holy Roman Church who is appointed by the Lord Pope for the Friars Minor, so that, always submissive and subject at the feet of that same Holy Church, and steadfast in the Catholic faith, we may perpetually observe the poverty and humility of Our Lord Jesus Christ and his most Holy Mother, and keep the commandments of the Holy Gospel, as we have faithfully promised. Amen.

Dated: Perugia, 16 September, in the tenth year of the pontificate of his Lordship Pope Innocent IV.[4]

Let no man on earth destroy this letter of confirmation or dare rashly to contravene it. If anyone shall presume to attempt such a thing, let him know that he will incur the indignation of Almighty God and his blessed Apostles, Peter and Paul.

Dated: Assisi, 9 August, in the eleventh year of our pontificate.[5]

NOTES

1 The Visitator was the official visitor, an office that originated with the Cistercians. His duty was to oversee the monastery. The first Visitator appointed for St Damian's was in fact a Cistercian; the second was a friar, Philip the Long; the third a secular.
2 The Cardinal Protector of the Order.
3 Clare insists on having material and spiritual assistance provided by the friars, as promised by Francis himself (an obligation which, after Francis' death, was increasingly disputed). In the early years of the Order these brothers lived beside the monasteries of the Poor Ladies. Innocent IV confirmed certain responsibilities of the friars towards the Poor Ladies in 1246 and his decision was reinforced in 1296 by Boniface VIII.
4 1252. The date of the approval of Cardinal Raynaldus dei Conti di Segni.
5 1253. The date of Innocent IV's approval of the Rule.

PART III

The Letters of St Clare
To Agnes of Prague

INTRODUCTION

The four letters of Clare to Agnes are probably for the modern reader the hardest of Clare's writings, but they are the heart. Profoundly mystical, densely allusive, packed with ecstatic outpourings and biblical references, they more than anything else yield up the special individuality of Clare. They are the fullest statement of her theology and her spirituality, and a clear illustration of her development of Franciscan thinking. Their style, consistently inspired, refined and lyrical, is quite unlike anything else in the saint's writings. Though these letters are addressed to another person, Clare speaks to us from the heart, and she emerges not just as a follower of Francis, but as someone who contributed much of her own in her realization of the gospel-centred life he had championed.

We know from the Life of Agnes of Prague that she corresponded with Clare. None of Agnes' letters survives, but we have four of Clare's (four of many, surely, for they were in touch over twenty years). Agnes was the daughter of King Ottakar I of Bohemia and his wife Queen Constance of Hungary (a cousin of St Elizabeth of Hungary). She was born in 1205, and engaged at the tender age of three to Boleslas of Silesia who died in 1211; then, in 1213, to the two-year-old son of Emperor Frederick II, who jilted her to marry the daughter of Duke Leopold of Austria. In 1227 Henry II of England offered to marry her, and in 1228 and again in 1233 Frederick II himself, whose wife had died, sued for her hand.

When the Friars Minor arrived in Prague in 1232, Agnes heard them preach and through them she must have learnt of Clare and St Damian's. She built the friars a church, then founded a hospital and attached to it a monastery. It was probably at this point that she wrote to Clare asking for help in establishing a convent of Poor Ladies. At Pentecost in 1234, with seven young noble ladies of her own country and five Poor Clares from Trento, she entered the monastery.

Clare's letters reveal a deep knowledge of the New Testament, and a good working knowledge of several books of the Old Testament, especially that book beloved of the Middle Ages, the Song of Solomon. Clare may not have been formally educated, but (assuming the letters are her own work – and we have no evidence whatever of reworking by secretaries) she displays a good grasp of the power of words, and of the balance and rhythms of periodic sentences, and she knows, perhaps instinctively, most of the stock-in-trade of conventional rhetoric. At moments she can rise to great heights of lyrical intensity, and at these moments her expressions seem irradiated with a mystical joy.

———

LETTER I
(DATED SOMETIME BEFORE 11 JUNE 1234)

[The dating of the letters is problematical. The first seems to have been written around the time when Agnes first entered religion. Possibly it may have been occasioned by the news that Agnes had rejected the suit of Frederick II and decided to live in poverty.]

To the venerable and most holy virgin, the Lady Agnes, daughter of the most excellent and illustrious King of Bohemia, Clare, the unworthy servant of Jesus Christ and unprofitable handmaid of the Enclosed Ladies of the monastery of St Damian, her subject and servant in all things, presents her humblest respects, with the special prayer that she attain the glory of eternal joy.[1]

Hearing reports of the perfect holiness of your[2] life and conduct, which is known not only to me, but has spread over almost all the world, I rejoice greatly and exult in the Lord. And it is not only I who rejoice at this, but all who serve and desire to serve Jesus Christ. For you, more than any other, could have chosen to enjoy all the pomp and honour and high offices of the world, and could have been the lawful wife of the illustrious Caesar[3] and crowned in regal splendour, as befitted your high station and his. But you have renounced all this, and with your whole heart and soul have chosen the life of most holy poverty and physical hardship. Thus you are taking a spouse of more noble lineage, the Lord Jesus Christ, who will always keep your virginity unspotted and intact.[4]

When you love him, you remain chaste; when you touch him, you will become more pure; when you accept him, you are still a virgin. For his power is mightier than any earthly power, his generosity greater, his countenance more fair, his love more sweet, his every grace more comely. You are already caught in his embrace, and he has adorned your breast with precious stones; upon your ears he has set pearls of untold value, and he has girded you about with gems sparkling like flowers in springtime, and crowned you with a golden crown marked with the emblem of sanctity.[5]

Therefore, dearest sister (or rather revered lady, for you are the bride, the mother and the sister of my Lord Jesus Christ,[6] and have been gloriously ennobled by the standard of inviolable virginity and most holy poverty), be strengthened in the holy service you have begun because of your ardent love for the poor crucified Christ, who for all our sakes endured the suffering of the cross, saving us from the power of the prince of darkness[7] by which we were held in bondage because of the disobedience of our first parent, and so reconciling us to God the Father.[8]

O blessed poverty, who gives eternal riches to those who love and embrace her! O holy poverty, since to those who possess her and long for her God promises the kingdom of heaven and offers the assurance of everlasting glory and a blessed life! O loving[9] poverty, which the Lord Jesus Christ, who ruled and still rules heaven and earth, who 'spake and it was done',[10] deigned to embrace above all else! For the foxes have holes, as he says, and the birds of the air their nests, but the Son of Man, Christ, has nowhere to lay his head;[11] but he bowed his head, and gave up the ghost.[12]

If, therefore, so great and merciful a Lord, born in a virgin's womb, chose to appear in the world as one despised, needy and poor, so that men, who were themselves so very poor and needy and suffering from a dire want of heavenly food, might become rich through him by possessing the kingdom of heaven, then shout for joy and be glad! Be filled with exceeding gladness and spiritual delight! For, having chosen contempt for the world rather than its honours, poverty rather than transient riches, and to lay up treasures in heaven rather than on earth, where there is no rust to consume, no moth to destroy, and no thieves to break in and steal it, your reward will be very great in heaven,[13] and you will have deserved most richly the right to be called the sister, bride and mother[14] of the Son of the Most High Father and of the glorious Virgin.

You know, I feel sure that the kingdom of heaven is promised and given only to the poor, for if we love earthly possessions we lose the fruits of love. It is not possible to serve God and Mammon, for either the one is loved and the other hated, or else a man will serve the one and despise the other.[15] And you know that one who is clothed cannot fight another who is naked, for if he offers the foe something to grasp, he is the more quickly thrown;[16] you also know that no-one can live in glory on earth and reign with Christ in heaven; and that a camel will be able to pass through the eye of a needle before a rich man can ascend to the kingdom of heaven.[17] Therefore you have cast aside your garments, that is, temporal riches, so that you may not be overwhelmed in your struggle against the foe, but may enter the kingdom of heaven by the straight path and by the narrow gate.[18]

What a wonderful and admirable exchange,[19] to abandon the things that perish for the things of eternity; to merit the blessings of heaven instead of those of the earth; to receive a hundredfold reward instead of one; and to possess a life of blessedness for ever!

For this reason I thought I must do all I could to beg you and humbly entreat you, most excellent and saintly sister, with all the tenderness of Christ, to fortify yourself in his holy service, progressing from good to better, from strength to strength, so that he whom you serve with all your heart's longing may deign to grant you the reward you desire.

I also beg you in the Lord, most earnestly, to remember me in your prayers, me your servant, however unworthy, and the other sisters in the monastery, who are all devoted to you. For thereby we may merit the mercy of Jesus Christ, and so, together with you, be found worthy to enjoy the everlasting vision.

Farewell in the Lord. And pray for me.

1 The language is formal and deferential, but conventional for the times, and Clare is addressing royalty. The extravagantly self-deprecatory phrases are very similar to those Francis used in his letters. The word translated as 'handmaid' (*ancilla*) is regularly used in religious literature to mean a cloistered woman who out of humility has chosen to be subordinate.

2 In this letter Clare uses the formal second person plural. In the other three letters she is more intimate.

3 The identity of the emperor is disputed. Probably it is Frederick II, who we know had asked for Agnes' hand in marriage.

4 The theme of mystical marriage of the virgin's soul with God is a leitmotiv of this and the fourth letter to Agnes. (The Song of Solomon, seen traditionally as an allegory of God's relationship with the Church, or the soul, is the book of the Bible most frequently alluded to in the Middle Ages.) For Clare, virginity did not mean self-denial: it meant fulfilment in the embrace of the Lord. Clare is at her most poetic and deeply spiritual when developing this theme. For her the mystical marriage was not to wait until death after a period of engagement spent in the cloister: it was the religious life itself.

5 Clare bases these lines on part of the Office for the Roman virgin martyr St Agnes (a special patroness of chastity, since she rejected marriage and consecrated her virginity to God).

6 Agnes is the 'mother' of Christ because devotion to and imitation of Mary implies spiritual motherhood. In the Office of the Passion Mary is called 'daughter and servant of the . . . Father of Heaven . . . Mother of Our Lord Jesus Christ, and the Beloved of the Holy Spirit'.

7 Compare Colossians 1.13.

8 Compare 2 Corinthians 5.18.

9 The Latin *pia* is a notoriously difficult word to translate. *Pietas* (which gave rise to both 'pity' and 'piety' in English) denotes a dutiful regard for our obligations to God and our family.

10 Compare Psalm 33.9.

11 Compare Matthew 8.20.

12 Compare John 19.30.

13 Compare Matthew 6.20 and 5.12.

14 Compare Matthew 12.50, and see above, note 6.

15 Matthew 6.24.

16 Compare Thomas of Celano *First Life*, ch. 15: 'And now Francis wrestled naked with his naked foe', an image taken from Gregory the Great's *Homilies on the Gospels* II 32.

17 Matthew 19.24.

18 Compare Matthew 7.13–14.

19 The exchange-motif is one favoured in Franciscan reflections on poverty. Compare Matthew 19.29. The Latin word *commercium* is here used of 'a bartering', 'a trading'.

———

LETTER II
(DATED BETWEEN 1234 AND 1239)

———

[Clare encourages Agnes (perhaps in the face of some difficulties) to persevere in her life of radical poverty. This letter may have been prompted by the efforts of Pope Gregory IX in 1235 to ensure that material provision was made for Agnes and her sisters. The question of material support for the monasteries of women was a matter which exercised him greatly. Later, in 1237, he allowed Agnes to go the way of St Damian's.]

To the Lady Agnes, daughter of the King of Kings, servant of the Lord of Lords, and most worthy spouse of Jesus Christ, and so most gentle queen, Clare, the worthless servant of the Poor Ladies, sends her greetings and the prayer that she may always live in the utmost poverty.[1]

I give thanks to the giver of grace, from whom, as we believe, every good gift and every perfect gift comes,[2] that he has adorned you with so many glorious virtues and graced you with the marks of such signal perfection that, having become a faithful follower of the Father, who is perfect, you may win grace to become perfect too, so that his eyes may see no imperfection in you.

This is that perfection with which the king himself will take you to his bosom in the heavenly bridal chamber where he sits in glory upon a starry throne,[3] because you have despised the glories of earthly power and counted the offers of an imperial

113

marriage of little worth; and having become a follower of utmost poverty in the spirit of great humility and most fervent charity, you have trod faithfully in the footprints of him to whom you have been found worthy to be joined in marriage.

Since I know of your many virtues I will be sparing with my words and not burden you with lengthy speeches, though I know you would not consider any writing overlong if it contained words of spiritual comfort. But because 'one thing alone is necessary',[4] I will bear witness to it now, and exhort you for the love of him to whom you have offered yourself as a holy and pleasing sacrifice, to remember always your vow, like another Rachel, ever mindful of what you have begun,[5] that you may keep what you have now and continue to do what you do now, and never abandon it, but press on at a swift pace, with light tread, without ever stumbling, so that your footsteps raise no worldly dust;[6] and that you may vigilantly forge ahead, passing securely and joyfully and speedily along the path of happiness, believing in nothing, agreeing with nothing that might keep you from your chosen path, or place a stumbling-block in your way and prevent you from fulfilling your vows to the Most High[7] in that fullness of perfection to which the Spirit of the Lord has called you.

But in all this, so that you may walk more securely in the way of the Lord's commandments, follow the counsel of our venerable father, Brother Elias,[8] the Minister General; value his counsel beyond that of any others, and think of it as the most precious gift you could possibly receive.

If anyone tells you something different[9] or suggests to you something else which would hinder your perfection or seems contrary to your divine calling, even if you are bound to show this person respect, do not follow his advice. As a poor virgin, hold fast to the poor Christ. Consider that he became contemptible for your sake and follow him, making yourself contemptible for him in this world. Your spouse is the most comely of the children of men, yet for your salvation he made himself the lowliest of men; he was despised, beaten, scourged many times over his whole body, then suffered the agony of the cross and died. Most noble queen, gaze upon him, consider him, contemplate him in your desire to imitate him.[10] If you suffer with him, you will reign with him; if you grieve with him, you will rejoice with him; if you die with him upon the cross of tribulation you will gain the heavenly mansions in the splendour of the saints, and your name will be written in the Book of Life[11] and be immortal among men. Because of this, for all eternity and world without end you will share the glory of the heavenly kingdom in place of perishable earthly things, and eternal bliss in place of passing pleasures, and you will live for ever.

Farewell, my dearest sister, and indeed my lady, because of the Lord, your spouse. Be sure to commend me and my sisters in your fervent prayers to the Lord, for we are all overjoyed at the good things the Lord is working in you through his grace. Please commend me to the prayers of all your sisters, also.

NOTES

1 Clare comes straight to the point of her letter: the life of poverty.
2 James 1.17.
3 From the liturgy (Second Antiphon at Lauds) of the Assumption of the Blessed Virgin Mary (15 August).
4 Luke 10.42.
5 Rachel (one of Laban's two daughters and the preferred wife of Jacob) was in the Middle Ages seen as the model of the contemplative life. Jerome interpreted her name as meaning 'seeing the beginning'.
6 Compare *First Life*, ch. 71. 'Dust' is symbolic of worldly contamination.
7 Psalm 50.14.
8 Elias was the third Minister General of the Order of Friars Minor. A controversial figure, he was deposed by Gregory IX in 1239, and later excommunicated and expelled from the Order.
9 Possibly a reference to Gregory IX's bull which attempted to make Agnes receive support for the maintenance of her community. In his Last Will, Francis is at pains to warn the Poor Ladies against false teaching.
10 The theme of imitation is crucial: consider the person of Christ, contemplate the poor Christ, desire to imitate his poverty, and you will be enabled to persevere in absolute poverty yourself. Another great woman saint, St Teresa of Avila, was to stress the importance of contemplating

the humanity of Christ. In chapter 22 of her autobiography she cites St Bernard, St Francis, St Antony of Padua and St Catherine of Siena as examples of contemplatives who 'rejoiced in the Humanity'.

11 Revelation 3.5.

LETTER III
(DATED 1238)

—

[A letter answering Agnes' request for clarification over some questions of fasting, which had possibly been occasioned by Gregory IX's bull of 1237 imposing total abstinence from meat on all Poor Ladies. But the letter should also be read against the background of the 1238 bull, addressed to the Damianites of Prague, in which the same pope officially accepted Agnes' decision to withdraw from the running of the Hospice of St Francis so that she could devote herself to a more contemplative life, without possessions or the burden of temporal concerns.]

To the lady most highly esteemed in Christ, and the sister whom I must love more than any other on earth, Agnes, sister[1] of the illustrious King of Bohemia, but now sister and spouse of the Almighty King of Heaven, Clare, most humble and unworthy handmaid of Christ and servant of the Poor Ladies, sends greetings, wishing her the joys of salvation in the Author of Salvation, and every good thing she can desire.

I am filled with such joy to hear of your good health, your happiness and splendid progress along the path you have undertaken to win the heavenly prize! And my spiritual joy is the more intense because I believe, indeed I know, that you are marvellously making amends for failures of mine and of the other sisters in following the footsteps of the poor and humble Jesus Christ.

Truly I am happy, and no-one can take this happiness from me,

116

since I now have what I desired most under heaven: I see that, aided by some special gift of grace proceeding from the mouth of God himself, you are in a quite amazing and unexpected way overthrowing the wiles of the cunning foe, the pride which deludes human nature and the vanity which leads human hearts astray. I see also that by your humility, by the power of your faith and poverty, you are holding tightly to that incomparable treasure hidden in the field of the world and of human hearts, which is the purchase-price of life with him[2] who created all things out of nothing. And, to use the actual words of the Apostle himself: I hold you to be a fellow-labourer with God,[3] and one who supports the failing members of his ineffable body.[4]

Who then would say that I do not have every reason to be overjoyed when I have so much to rejoice over? So you, too, must rejoice in the Lord, my dearest daughter. Let no bitterness or sadness cloud your joy, O most beloved lady in Christ, joy of the angels, and crown of your sisters! Place your spirit before the mirror[5] of eternity; place your soul before the splendour of God's glory; place your heart before the image of the divine essence[6] and, through contemplation, transform yourself entirely into the likeness of God himself, so that you too may feel what his friends feel when they taste the hidden sweetness which God has reserved from the very beginning for those who love him. Shun utterly all those things that[7] in a deceitful and troubled world can win the affection of the unseeing, and love totally the one who gave himself totally for love of you; he at whose beauty the sun and moon wonder, the preciousness and lavishness of whose rewards are unending.[8] I speak of him who is the Son of the Most High, whom the Virgin brought forth and after his birth remained a virgin. Cling fast to his modest, sweet mother, who gave birth to a son whom the heavens could not contain, yet whom she carried in the tiny enclosure of her holy womb and held on her maidenly lap. Who would not shrink in terror from the treacheries of the enemy of man, who through the arrogance of momentary and deceptive glories would try to reduce to nothing what is

117

greater than heaven itself? For it is indeed clear that through God's grace the soul of a faithful man, the most worthy of all creatures, is greater than heaven, since the heavens and all the rest of creation together cannot contain their Creator, and only the faithful soul can be his abode and throne, and this only through the charity that the sinful lack. For he who is Truth says: 'He that loveth me shall be loved of my Father . . . and we will come unto him and make our abode with him.'[9] So, as the glorious Virgin of Virgins carried him physically, in her body, so you too, by following in her footsteps, imitating especially her humility and poverty, can without any doubt always carry him spiritually in your chaste and virginal body,[10] holding within yourself the one by whom you and all creation are held together, possessing that which, by comparison with the other transitory possessions of this world, you will possess more steadfastly. In this respect some earthly kings and queens are deluded: for though their pride reaches up to the skies and their heads touch the clouds, in the end they are worth no more than the dung-heap.[11]

Now, as regards those matters which you have asked me to explain to you. You want to know about the feast days which our most glorious father St Francis ordered us to celebrate in a special way by a relaxation of our fasting. I think you are more or less familiar with them already, but nonetheless, dearest sister, I thought I should answer you.

You should be aware of the following: except for sisters who are weak and infirm, for whom St Francis urged and required us to show the greastest possible consideration in the matter of their food, none of us who are healthy and well should eat anything but the food prescribed for Lent, whether on ferias or on feast days, and we must fast[12] every day except Sundays and Christmas Day, when we are to eat two meals. On ordinary Thursdays sisters may do as they wish, and no-one who does not wish to fast is obliged to do so. However, those of us who are well fast every day except for Sundays and Christmas Day. During the whole of Easter Week, as Francis tells us in what he has written,[13] and on

118

the feasts of the Blessed Virgin Mary and the Holy Apostles, we are not obliged to fast unless those feast days occur on a Friday. And, as I have already said, we who are healthy and strong always eat what is prescribed for Lent.

But seeing that our flesh is not flesh of bronze nor our strength a strength of stone,[14] but on the contrary that we are frail and prone to every bodily weakness, I beseech you, dearest daughter, and I beg you in the Lord, to show wisdom and good sense and give up that unwise and excessive rigour in fasting which I know you have taken upon yourself, that you may live to praise the Lord and to offer him a service that is reasonable,[15] and that your sacrifice may always be seasoned with salt.[16]

Farewell, and may you always prosper in the Lord, as I hope to do myself. Please remember me and my sisters in your prayers.

NOTES

1 King Ottakar I had died in 1230. Agnes' brother Vaclav III was now king.
2 The Latin has neuter *illud* ('that thing', 'that essence'), but clearly the meaning is 'God', so I have translated with a masculine pronoun.
3 Compare 1 Corinthians 3.9.
4 Referring to the contribution of the contemplative life in the mission of the Church.
5 On the 'mirror of contemplation' image, which is widespread in the spiritual literature of the twelfth and thirteenth centuries, see below on the fourth letter to Agnes, note 8.
6 Compare Hebrews 1.3.
7 Reading *quae* for *qui*.
8 Here and in the next few lines Clare is using words from (a) the liturgy of the feast of St Agnes, 21 January, and (b) the Feast of the Annunciation, 25 March.
9 Compare John 14. 21, 23.
10 On spiritual motherhood see above on first letter to Agnes, note 6.
11 Medieval writers were less squeamish than we are. Compare Philippians 3.8; the same phrase occurs in the Lives of Barlaam and Josaphat in the *Golden Legend* (Penguin edn, p. 356).
12 On fasting see *Legend*, chapter 18, note 4; *Rule* ch. 3. Clare reiterates Francis' practices, but says nothing of the pope's new total ban on meat.
13 Francis' pronouncements have unfortunately not survived. He does not refer to these times in either of his Rules.

14 Compare Job 6.12.

15 Romans 12.1. 'Reasonable service' in the sense of 'the homage it is right to offer God', 'the worship due from us as rational creatures'.

16 See Leviticus 2.13. Presumably this is the salt of wisdom and discretion.

LETTER IV
(DATED BETWEEN FEBRUARY AND
THE BEGINNING OF AUGUST 1253)

[A letter written near the end of Clare's life. Of all that survive this letter is the most personal and affectionate. In it Clare returns to the theme of mystical marriage, taking St Agnes the virgin martyr as the model, the perfect bride of Christ, and quoting from the Office of the saint (21 January). As she writes to Agnes lyrically of the ultimate embrace with the Beloved, Clare is no doubt reflecting on her own death and the final fulfilment of her life of holiness. There is a strong focus on death and martyrdom.]

To the one who is half of her soul and the sanctuary of her heart's most special love, the Lady Agnes, illustrious queen and bride of the Lamb,[1] the Eternal King, her beloved mother and most special daughter of all, Clare, unworthy servant of Christ and worthless handmaid of his handmaids in the monastery of St Damian, Assisi, sends greetings, with the prayer that, together with the other most holy virgins, she may sing a new song before the throne of God and follow the Lamb wherever he shall go.[2]

O my mother and daughter, bride of the King of All Ages, though I have not written as often as your heart and mine desire and could wish, do not be surprised, and do not imagine for a moment that the fire of love for you burns less brightly in your mother's breast. The problem is the lack of messengers and the obvious dangers of the roads. Now, however, dearest sister, I am

120

writing to you, and I rejoice with you, I exult with you in the joy of the Spirit,[3] O bride of Christ, because having dispensed with all the vanities of this world you have, like that other most holy virgin Agnes, become most marvellously wedded to the Spotless Lamb[4] who takes away the sins of the world.

Happy is she, indeed, to whom it is given to enjoy this sacred banquet, so that she may cling with all her heart's desire to him whose beauty all the blessed armies of the skies admire without ceasing; whose love arouses our love; whose contemplation refreshes the soul; whose kindness fills us with joy; whose sweetness satiates us; whose remembrance dawns in us with delight; at whose fragrance the dead shall be revived;[5] whose glorious vision shall bless all the citizens of the heavenly Jerusalem, since this is the splendour of eternal glory, the radiance of eternal light, and the mirror without flaw.[6]

Look into this mirror every day, O Queen, O Bride of Jesus Christ, and there continually gaze upon your face, that thus you may adorn and array your whole being, both inwardly and outwardly, in the richest robes, and deck yourself in the flowers and the garments of all the virtues as befits the daughter and most chaste[7] spouse of the Most High King. Poverty, holy humility and ineffable charity are reflected in this mirror, as you will see for yourself, with God's grace, as you gaze at the whole surface of the mirror.

First look at the outer edge[8] of this mirror, at the poverty of him who was placed in a manger and wrapped in mean swaddling clothes. O wondrous humility! O amazing poverty! The King of angels, the Lord of heaven and earth lies in a manger! Then, in the middle of the mirror, consider the humility and the blessed poverty, the countless labours and pains he endured for the redemption of the human race. Finally, in the lower depths of this same mirror, contemplate the indescribable love with which he chose to suffer on the wood of the cross and to die the most shameful death imaginable. And so that Mirror, hung upon the wood of the cross, urged all who passed along the way to consider: 'O all ye who pass by, behold and see if there is any sorrow like unto my sorrow.'[9] So let us reply with one voice and one spirit to him as he groans and cries out: 'My spirit will ponder it continually, and my soul shall languish within me.'[10]

Therefore, O Queen of the heavenly King, may your heart be inflamed more and more with the fervour of this love! And as you go on to contemplate his ineffable delights, the riches and eternal honours he offers, and as you sigh for them in the boundless desire and love of your heart, cry out: 'Draw me after you, and we will run after the fragrance of your perfumes,[11] heavenly spouse! I shall run and never weary, until you bring me into the banqueting hall, until your left hand cradles my head and your right hand embraces me in happiness,[12] and you kiss me with the most happy kiss of your lips!'[13]

In the midst of this contemplation remember your poor little mother, knowing that I have inscribed the happy memory of you indelibly on the tablets of my heart,[14] because I hold you dearer than all others.

What more can I say? The mortal tongue must be silent in speaking of my love for you, and I must speak the language of the spirit. O my blessed daughter, since no fleshly tongue could fully express the love I bear for you, I beg you to accept with kindness and devotion what I have written so inadequately, recognizing in it at least the motherly love which burns every day in my heart for you and your daughters, to whom please commend me and my daughters in Christ most warmly. My own daughters, and especially the most prudent virgin Agnes, my own sister, send greetings, and beg you and your daughters most earnestly to remember them in their prayers.

Farewell, dearest daughter, to you and your daughters until we meet before the glorious throne of the great God.[15] Pray to him for us.

The bearers of this letter are our dearest brothers Amatus, beloved of God and men, and Bonagura,[16] both of whom I commend to you warmly and without reservation. Amen.

1 St Agnes is often pictured with a lamb, a play on the Latin word for lamb (*agnus*). Perhaps significantly, St Agnes is the only saint named by Clare in her writings, and in making this reference she underlines her close relationship with Agnes of Prague.

2 Compare Revelation 14.4.

3 Compare 1 Thessalonians 1.6.

4 Agnes has become wedded to the Agnus Dei, the Lamb of God.

5 Pseudo-Ambrose, Epistle 1.

6 Wisdom 7.26. Here the important mirror-theme is revived: for Clare to reflect on Jesus, and to reflect him, was an attitude of life.

7 Reading *castissima* for *carissima*.

8 'Outer surface ... centre ... depths': the mirrors of medieval times were bronze discs, convex on one side, which reflected more or less distorted images depending on where the gaze was directed upon the curve of the surface (see *Early Documents*, p. 50, note d). Here Clare refers to the beginning, middle and end of Christ's earthly life as reflected in different areas of the mirror surface. It is difficult, if not impossible, to bring out both ideas in intelligible English.

9 Lamentations 1.12. As she nears death Clare focuses more and more on the cross and on identification with Christ.

10 Lamentations 3.20.

11 Song of Solomon 1.3–4. In a series of quotations from this book Clare seems inebriated at the thought of the ultimate embrace with the Beloved.

12 Compare Song of Solomon 2.4; 2.6.

13 Compare Song of Solomon 1.1 (Vulgate); 1.2 (AV).

14 Proverbs 3.3.

15 A clear note of leave-taking: Clare is dying.

16 A play on words. Latin *Amatus* means 'beloved', and *Bonaugura* would mean 'good wishes'. Neither of these brothers can be identified.

123

INDEX

⌐——

Numbers in brackets refer to notes

abbess, title of xv, 22, 24(2)
   election of 91f, 93(1)
   office of 52, 52(1), 83, 87f, 88(1), 90,
   91, 91(3), 93(2), 98, 99, 100
abstinence *see* fasting
Acre xxi
Acta Sanctorum 33(8)
Acts, Book of 72(4)
Admonition of sisters 100
Agnes of Prague, Blessed x, xv, xix, 14(7),
   21(12), 26(6), 30(6), 51(3), 63(11),
   107f, 109, 115(9), 116, 120, 123(1,4)
   letters to 105–23
Agnes, sister of St Clare xv, xx, 37–9,
   39(1,2,5), 57, 60(2), 62, 63(11), 122
Agnes, Sister (daughter of mayor of Assisi)
   24(4), 60(12)
Alessandrina of Fratta 66, 67(2)
Alexander IV, Pope viii, xviii, 6(5), 7(12),
   54(8), 76, 77(1), 83, 86(2)
All Saints, Feast of 90
alms 96f
Amata of Corozano, Sister 43(7), 47,
   48(6)
Amatus, Brother 122, 123(10)
Anagni xviii, 77, 78(8)
Andrea da Ferrara, Sister 73, 74(4)
Angela of Foligno 24(4), 42(1,3)
Angelo Tancredi, Brother 7(11), 58, 60(7),
   78(3), 78(6)
Annunciation, feast of 119(8)
Assisi vii, xii, xiii, 33, 34(1), 35(6), 37(1),
   54, 54(11), 62(4), 68, 69(1), 72(6),
   72(10), 74, 75(3), 78(3), 104
Assumption of Blessed Virgin Mary 48,
   90, 115(3), 119

Bartholomew of Spoleto, Bishop viii, ix,
   xvii, 14(5), 78(3)
Bartoli, Marco xxiv, 12(5), 51(3)
Basilica of St Clare, Assisi 20(6), 39(5),
   63(10)
Basilica of St Francis, Assisi 54(11)
Bastia xiv, 17(13)
Beatrice, sister of St Clare 14(4), 26(3),
   39(1)
Beguines xiv, 91(4), 97(2)
Benedict XIV, Pope 39(5)

Benvenuta, Sister, of Lady Diambra, 47,
   48(5)
Benvenuta, Sister, of Perugia 30(2), 48
Bernardone, Giovanni di Pietro xii
Bettona 70, 72(1)
Bevagna 72, 72(10), 75(3)
Beziers xxi
Bohemia, King of
   Ottakar I x, 107, 109
   Vaclav III 116, 119(1)
Boleslaus of Silesia 107
Bollandists 52(3)
Bologna 54(4)
Bona de Guelfuccio 14(4)
Bona of Monte Galliano 74, 75(1)
Bonagura, Brother 122, 123(16)
Boniface VIII, Pope 104(3)
'Book of Life' 115, 116(11)
Bruges xxi
Bulls
   '*Clara claris praeclara*' 78(5)
   '*Gloriosus Deus*' 78(3)
   '*Quo Elongati*' 51(4)
   '*Solet annuere*' xvii, 57(5), 82
Buongiovanni Martini 69

Cannara 75, 75(3)
canon law 91, 93(1)
'Canticle of Brother Sun' xvi
Cardinal Protector *see* Protector
Carney, Margaret, OSF 84
Caterina, sister of St Clare xiv, 39(1)
Catholic Poor Men xiii
Cecilia, Sister 27(3)
chaplain 103
Chapter, meetings of 92
Chapter of Paris 78(6)
chastity, ideal of 86, 112(4,5)
Christmas 90, 91(2)
Cistercians 104(1)
Clare, St
   accepts title of abbess 22
   asks Innocent III for Privilege of
   Poverty 25
   baptism 10, 10(8)
   beauty 12(7)
   birth vii, xi, 9
   canonization of viii, xviii, 4, 76f

124

obedience
  owed to abbess 100
  probationer received into 88
  promised by Poor Ladies to St Francis 86f, 95
  to Cardinal Protector 103
Office of St Agnes 112(5), 120
Office of St Clare xxi
Office of the Cross (= Office of the Passion) 45(6), 89(10)
Office of the Dead 61, 90
Office, Divine, recitation of 90, 90–1(1), 94
Office of Virgins 61
Offreduccio family xi, xii
Orders
  Order of Friars Minor xx, 78(6), 91, 102, 103, 107, 115(8)
  Second Order (of Poor Ladies) xx, 21, 22(4), 25, 96(3)
organ(s) 43(4)
Ortolana (mother of Clare)
  enters Order 47
  feast day of 48(4)
  meaning of name 10(4), 48(4)
  piety of xi, 9f
  prophecy concerning birth of Clare vii, 10, 43(6)
Ostia 86(2)
Ostia, Bishop of
  (= Hugolino) 40
  (= Hugolino's nephew, Raynaldus of Segni) 53, 54(8), 61, 62(5), 85, 86(2), 104(4)
Ottakar I, King of Bohemia x, 107, 109, 119(1)

Pacifica, Sister 49(10)
Padua xv, 39(5)
Pamplona xxi
parlour 93, 94(3), 103
paternosters, recitation of 90
penance 21, 99
penitential movement 30(1)
Pennacchi, Francesco xxiv, 62(3)
Pentecost 90
Perugia xii, 47, 48, 53, 54(4), 66, 69, 73, 103
Petriolo of Bettona 70
Philippians, Epistle to 14(7), 119(11)
Philip the Long, Brother, of Atri xiv, 50, 51(1), 104(1)
Piazza San Rufino, Assisi xi
Pisa 40
Pius XII, Pope 43(6)
Plenaria of Bevagna 72
Podesta 61, 62(1)
Poland xxi
Poor Ladies (of Saints Cosmas and Damian) ix, xv, xvi, xix, xx, 20(8), 81, 87(1), 104(3)
Portiuncula xiii, xiv, xvi, 12(2), 16, 17(7), 52(3), 63(9)
portress 101
poverty
  ideal of 26(2), 86, 110f, 113, 115(1)
  vow of 95f, 97
Prague x, xv, 83, 107
'Praises of the Virtues' 26(2)
'Prayer of Five Wounds of Our Lord' 45(5), 60(12)
Prime 90
privilege of poverty x, 25, 26(8), 54, 54(10), 81
probation 88
Process of Canonization viii, 3, 6(1), 7(12), 12(2,5), 14(4), 17(9), 24(4), 26(3), 27(3), 28(2), 30(2,4), 33(13), 32–3(7), 33(10), 37(1), 42(1), 43–4(7), 48(2), 48–9(7), 49(10), 57(5), 60(12), 65(4), 78(3)
procurator 92, 93(5)
profession, formula of 87(2), 88f
property, possession of 96, 97
Protector of Poor Ladies xviii, 6(3), 27(10), 54(8), 87, 88(2), 102, 104(2)
Protomonastery of St Clare 82
Proverbs, Book of 12(2), 123(14)
Psalms, Book of xxiv, 22(1), 60(12), 112(10), 115(7)
Pseudo-Ambrose 123(5)

questors 27(11), 28

Rachel 114, 115(5)
Raynaldo, Brother 58
Raynaldus, Cardinal (later Pope Alexander IV) see Bishop of Ostia
refectorian 27, 27(1)
refectory 92, 93, 94(2), 99
'Reformers' 78(6)
relics, theft of 62(3)
'requiem aeternam' 90
Revelation, Book of 24(2), 49(11), 60(10), 116(11), 123(2)
Rheims xxi
Rieti 69(4)
Romans, Epistle to 12(6), 28(1), 56(1), 120(15)
Rome 78(7)
Rule
  Early Rule of Francis 119(13)
  Later (official) Rule of Francis xvii, 50(3), 51(4), 81f, 101(2), 119(13)
  of Augustine x
  of Benedict x, 32(7), 81, 93(4)
  of Clare ix, xv, xvi, xvii, xix, xx,